WHAT WAS SHAKESPEARE REALLY LIKE?

Sir Stanley Wells is one of the world's greatest authorities on William Shakespeare. Here he brings a lifetime of learning and reflection to bear on some of the most tantalizing questions about the poet and dramatist that there are. How did he think, feel, and work? What were his relationships like? What did he believe about death? What made him laugh? This freshly thought and immensely engaging study wrestles with fundamental debates concerning Shakespeare's personality and life. The mysteries of how Shakespeare lived, whom and how he loved, how he worked, how he produced some of the greatest and most abidingly popular works in the history of world literature and drama, have fascinated readers for centuries. This concise, crystalline book conjures illuminating insights to reveal Shakespeare as he was. Wells brings the writer and dramatist alive, in all his fascinating humanity, for readers of today.

PROFESSOR SIR STANLEY WELLS, CBE, FRSL, is Honorary President of the Shakespeare Birthplace Trust. His many books include *Shakespeare: For All Time* (2002), *Looking for Sex in Shakespeare* (2004), *Shakespeare & Co.* (2006), *Shakespeare, Sex, and Love* (2010) and *Great Shakespeare Actors* (2015). He edited *Shakespeare Survey* for almost twenty years, and is co-editor of *The Cambridge Companion to Shakespeare on Stage* (with Sarah Stanton, 2002), *The New Cambridge Companion to Shakespeare* (with Margreta de Grazia, 2010), *The Shakespeare Circle: An Alternative Biography* (with Paul Edmondson, 2015) and *All the Sonnets of Shakespeare* (with Paul Edmondson, 2020). He is also General Editor of the Oxford and Penguin editions of Shakespeare.

What Was Shakespeare Really Like?

Stanley Wells

With a foreword by Stephen Fry

CAMBRIDGE
UNIVERSITY PRESS

CAMBRIDGE
UNIVERSITY PRESS

Shaftesbury Road, Cambridge CB2 8EA, United Kingdom

One Liberty Plaza, 20th Floor, New York, NY 10006, USA

477 Williamstown Road, Port Melbourne, VIC 3207, Australia

314–321, 3rd Floor, Plot 3, Splendor Forum, Jasola District Centre, New Delhi – 110025, India

103 Penang Road, #05–06/07, Visioncrest Commercial, Singapore 238467

Cambridge University Press is part of Cambridge University Press & Assessment, a department of the University of Cambridge.

We share the University's mission to contribute to society through the pursuit of education, learning and research at the highest international levels of excellence.

www.cambridge.org
Information on this title: www.cambridge.org/9781009340373
DOI: 10.1017/9781009340403

First published 2023

Printed in the United Kingdom by CPI Group Ltd, Croydon CR0 4YY

A catalogue record for this publication is available from the British Library.

A Cataloging-in-Publication data record for this book is available from the Library of Congress

ISBN 978-1-009-34037-3 Hardback

CONTENTS

ILLUSTRATIONS

FOREWORD
Stephen Fry

The Forest of Arden is as nothing to the impenetrable thickets of Shakespearean scholarship that so often block out the light, choking the paths and entangling generations of schoolchildren who are expected to hack their way through. How often do we hear 'Shakespeare was ruined for me at school'? For many, his works are for 'other people', for – to use the most grievous insult of our age – the cultural elite.

It was never so in Shakespeare's own time, of course. He was the most popular (and financially successful) dramatist of his day; his histories, tragedies, and comedies delighted contemporary audiences of all sorts and conditions. If one wanted to do so, one could compare him to ... Peter Morgan, say, the creator of the Netflix series *The Crown*, and to ... I don't know ... Julian Fellowes of *Gosford Park*, or to Ricky Gervais, Steven Spielberg, and the creators of the Marvel Cinematic Universe – but such comparisons are only ways of restating Shakespeare's *reach*, they say nothing of the particular qualities that have elevated him to the unique status he has attained around the world for the best part of four hundred years. He combined all the excellence of the most popular and skilled creators of dramatic entertainment we can think of, but with a depth, scale, and poetic power and insight that no playwright, novelist, film director, or screenwriter has since come close to.

The poet Robert Graves juicily observed that 'the remarkable thing about Shakespeare is that he is really very good – in spite of all the people who say he is very good'. And how people do beat the drum for his greatness. He and his works are famous for exhausting superlatives, and tiresome declamations of his genius (like mine) are of no help. Such 'bardolatry' only makes the frustration (and often anger and contempt) of those who 'don't get him' all the more intense.

The Nobel Prize laureate Richard Feynman, one of the greatest physicists of the twentieth century, was celebrated for the way he could explain the most impenetrable and profound ideas in science to anyone. Rare as the gift of understanding the mathematical and conceptual complexities of physics might be, the gift of being able to *communicate* them is rarer still. And so it is in the field of Shakespeare Studies. Shakespeare may not be as difficult as quantum mechanics, but some seem to go out of their way to make him so.

Forward Professor Sir Stanley Wells, whose knowledge and scholarship are equal to any academic anywhere, but whose ability to talk and write straightforwardly, clearly, and revealingly about all aspects of Shakespeare is absolutely unequalled. Over a long and fruitful life he has, to mangle Cassius, bestridden the field like a colossus. It is, I think, incontestable to claim that no single person in history has done more for the study and appreciation of Shakespeare.

The four chapters in this book ask four beguilingly simple questions which result in deeply fascinating and exciting journeys into Shakespeare's mind and practice. As you read, you are very likely to exclaim, as I did, 'Why the hell didn't my English teacher talk like this?'

The final Epilogue takes us on a delightful excursion through the eight decades that Sir Stanley has spent helping the world understand Shakespeare better as creator, person, and phenomenon. Actors, directors, producers, lecturers, teachers, students, and all who want to know and understand more will hug this book to them.

We could say of Stanley Wells what Matthew Arnold says of William Shakespeare:

> Others abide our question. Thou art free.
> We ask and ask – Thou smilest and art still,
> Out-topping knowledge.[1]

---

1 *The Poems of Matthew Arnold*, C. B. Tinker and H. F. Lowry (eds). Oxford University Press, 1950, p. 2

PREFACE

This little book contains the lightly revised text of four lectures which I was invited to write for delivery in the Shakespeare Centre, headquarters of the Shakespeare Birthplace Trust, Stratford-upon-Avon, in April and May 2020 to celebrate my ninetieth birthday, on 21 May of that year. Because of the pandemic, however, they were instead delivered online, at weekly intervals. They were edited and recorded, in somewhat shortened form, in my home with the indispensable editorial and technical help of the Head of Research at the Shakespeare Birthplace Trust, Dr Paul Edmondson, to whom this little book is gratefully dedicated. Each lecture was generously introduced by a friend, Professors Russell Jackson and Michael Dobson, both of whom had studied with me and went on to follow me as director of the Shakespeare Institute of the University of Birmingham; Gregory Doran, artistic director of the Royal Shakespeare Company, of which I am honorary governor emeritus; and Professor Lena Orlin, trustee of the Shakespeare Birthplace Trust, of which I am honorary president. The lectures were made available through the trust's website, www.shakespeare.org.uk, with the accidental (but, for me, happy) result that many more people in many different countries heard them than if they had been given in person, as originally intended. For this printed version I have restored passages omitted in the recording and made a few revisions.

The Cobbe Portrait of William Shakespeare. Copyright The
Cobbe Collection. See pp. 133–4.

1   *What Manner of Man Was He?*

I n this book I want to think about four specific aspects of Shakespeare's life and work. In this first chapter I shall discuss the general problem of discerning the personality of a writer who spent a lifetime of creative activity in depicting people other than himself. In the second chapter I shall address the question of how Shakespeare set about the task of writing a play. Thirdly, I shall ask what we can deduce about his personality from the body of work in which he seems to write most directly about himself, his sonnets. And finally I shall ask what made him laugh.

First, how can we hope to know what he was like? It's a question that characters in his plays ask about other characters. When a nobleman intrudes upon the revels in the Boar's Head Tavern (*1 Henry IV*, 2. 5.295), Sir John Falstaff asks 'What manner of man is he?' In the same scene (lines 422–423) Prince Hal asks Falstaff, who is standing in for King Henry, 'What manner of man, an it like your majesty?' In *Twelfth Night*, Olivia, referring to the disguised Viola, asks Malvolio first 'What kind o' man is he?' then 'What manner of man?' (1.5.145, 147); in *As You Like It* Rosalind asks 'what manner of man' is Orlando (3.2.201). And in *The Winter's*

Tale the Clown asks Autolycus 'What manner of fellow was he that robbed you?' (4.4.84).

The question, natural enough at any time and in any place, is especially relevant to a dramatist seeking to depict human beings in real-life situations (rather than, for example, the stylized abstractions of the morality plays). It would have been familiar to Shakespeare's audiences not least from the words of St Mark about Jesus in the King James Bible, 'What manner of man is this that even the winds and the sea obey him?' (Matthew 8: 27). The clear implication here is that he – Jesus – is some sort of superman. Modern colloquial equivalents relating to ordinary mortals are 'What makes her tick?' and 'What sort of a chap is he?'

The question has provoked a whole school, or technique, of criticism based on the attempt to define and analyze characters within the plays, and to discuss their origins, even to portray the girlhoods of their heroines, on the basis of what they say, and do, and on what is said about them, as if they were real people. The method, often associated especially with the late-Victorian critic A. C. Bradley, has provoked dispute as well as agreement, and was famously mocked by L. C. Knights in his 1933 essay 'How Many Children Had Lady Macbeth?' Bradley himself has a substantial and deeply thoughtful (if ponderously expressed) essay called 'Shakespeare the Man' in his *Oxford Lectures on Poetry*, first published in 1909, in which he sounds somewhat defensive about the enterprise: he writes that 'the natural desire to know whatever can be known of him is not to be repressed merely because there are people so foolish as to be careless about his works and yet curious about his private life'(p. 243). There is,

I suspect, a covert reference here to contemporary responses, such as those of Oscar Wilde and Samuel Butler, to homosexual readings of Shakespeare's sonnets. And Bradley confesses that 'though I should care nothing about the man if he had not written the works, yet, since we possess them, I would rather see and hear him for five minutes in his proper person than discover a new one' (p. 243). A rather odd admission: would you swap, say, the lost *Love's Labour's Won*, or even the joint-authored, and also lost, *Cardenio*, for five minutes with Shakespeare, possibly on a bad day?

Bradley continues: 'And though we may be content to die without knowing his income or even the surname of Mr W. H.' – to whom the publisher Thomas Thorpe dedicated the 1609 collection of sonnets – 'we cannot so easily resign the wish to find the man in the writings, and to form some idea of the disposition, the likes and dislikes, the character and the attitude towards life, of the human being who seems to us to have understood best our common human natures' (p. 313). The wish expressed here is predictable since Bradley is associated especially with character-based criticism – the attempt to write and to talk about the characters of Shakespeare's plays as if they were real people, and the tendency to value his plays especially for their psychological insights into human character.

It is natural to apply the question What was he really like? not only to characters in Shakespeare's plays but also to the author of the plays in which these characters appear. But it is not easily answered. A narrative account of the bare facts of a person's journey through life, their parentage and education, their career, the 'actions that a man might play' (*Hamlet*,

1.2.84) do not, as Hamlet knows, pluck out the heart of his mystery. A curriculum vitae or a *Who's Who* entry may supply such an account. What people show to the world around them may reveal little or nothing of their inner being, just as the visible signs of Hamlet's mourning for Claudius are 'but the trappings and the suits of woe' (*Hamlet*, 1.2.86).

Biographical studies of Shakespeare vary in the degree to which they attempt to dig below the surface to interpret the facts of his life in search of the inner man. Some accounts are pretty well wholly objective. I think for example of E. K. Chambers's *William Shakespeare: A Study of Facts and Problems*, published in 1930, and of S. Schoenbaum's *Shakespeare: A Documentary Life* (1977), and its lesser-known sequel, *Records and Images* (1981), which offer raw materials for the biography that Schoenbaum hoped to write but did not live long enough to accomplish. At the other extreme is Katherine Duncan-Jones's *Shakespeare: An Ungentle Life* (2001; revised 2014). It's a combative title. She is picking up on the fact that several of Shakespeare's contemporaries, including Ben Jonson, referred to him as 'gentle' (which could refer to social status, as in 'gently born', no less than to character. In Shakespeare's time a gentleman was a man entitled to display a coat of arms). In Duncan-Jones's view, the adjective as applied to his character is undeserved. Making interpretative use of absence of evidence, she remarks in the blurb of her book that 'unlike other local worthies, or his actor-contemporary Edward Alleyn', Shakespeare 'shows no inclination to divert any of his wealth towards charitable, neighbourly or altruistic ends'. This is not really fair, since he left £10 – no small sum, amounting to half of the local schoolmaster's annual salary – to the poor of Stratford, and there are also bequests to neighbours and to other persons outside the immediate family circle.

There have also been attempts – less fashionable now than previously – to apply the techniques of psychoanalysis to Shakespeare through interpretation of both the life records and the works. An example is the volume entitled *Shakespeare's Personality* (1989), edited by Norman N. Holland and other scholars, which offers a series of essays, many of them based on Freudian psychology, relating Shakespeare's life to his works. Its index includes entries for such subjects as Shakespeare's 'abhorrence of vagina', his 'compliant tendencies', his 'erotic versus aggressive drives', his 'phallic fantasy', his 'sexual fantasies', and his 'vindictive impulses'.

For all its intellectual sophistication, such work has to negotiate two difficult obstacles. One is our imperfect knowledge of the facts of Shakespeare's life. For instance, several of the contributors to Holland's volume make much of what the editor refers to in his introduction as Shakespeare's 'father's loss of patriarchal authority as a result of his financial decline' (p. 7). But that supposed financial decline is imperfectly documented and has indeed been disputed in a study by David Fallow (*The Shakespeare Circle*, pp. 34–36). John Shakespeare was buried in September 1601; William, who already owned New Place, was his eldest son and clearly inherited John's house, now known as the Birthplace, in Henley Street; only nine months later William made the most expensive purchase of his life, paying £320 for a large area of land in Old Stratford and on the Welcombe Hills. I should be surprised if all this money came from his theatrical earnings. If his father's supposed financial decline didn't occur, theories of its supposed psychological effect on Shakespeare are invalidated.

A major obstacle to reading Shakespeare's life through his plays is the fact that they are not purely the product of his own imagination but draw heavily both for their plots and their language on historical events and on writings by other people, and so cannot be properly thought of as purely the projections of his subconscious mind or as reflections of his personal experience. To give an example close to home – in more than one sense – there is a speech in *Henry IV, Part Two* written about the time that Shakespeare was buying and, there is reason to believe, renovating New Place in which it is tempting to suppose that he was drawing on recent personal experience:

> When we mean to build
> We first survey the plot, then draw the model;
> And when we see the figure of the house,
> Then must we rate the cost of the erection,
> Which if we find outweighs ability,
> What do we then but draw anew the model
> In fewer offices, or, at least, desist
> To build at all?   (1.3.41–48)

The temptation to see these lines as autobiographical may dwindle, however, when we find that they paraphrase quite closely the Parable of the Wise and Foolish Builder in St Matthew's Gospel, 7: 24–27.

Attempts like those in the Holland volume to offer an interpretation of the external evidence in the hope of defining what Shakespeare was like must delve beneath the exterior facts in endeavouring to define the essentials of his personality, what makes him different from other men, what characterizes his attitude to his fellow human beings and the way in which he reacts to the situations in which he finds himself, qualities such as his sense of humour, his tenacity, his conscientiousness, his predictability, his temperament, his sensibility, his sexuality, his attitudes to the great questions of life and death, his spirituality, his moral stances, and his imaginative makeup. For the Elizabethans, these qualities were determined by the four bodily humours – black bile, yellow bile, phlegm, and blood – which in turn influenced the four basic temperaments – choleric, phlegmatic, melancholic, and sanguine. Such simplistic, rough and ready categorizations offer mere pigeon-holes into which people can be slotted with little regard for true individuality. Attempts at definition of character demand far more subtlety; they must acknowledge too that personality is not constant, that people change and develop over the years, and that appetites alter – that, as Benedick says in *Much Ado About Nothing*, a man may love 'the meat in his youth that he cannot endure in his age' (2.3.226–227).

Are there, in spite of the many notorious gaps in our knowledge about Shakespeare's life, the paucity of personal documentation, the absence of self-revelatory letters such as we have for John Keats, of diaries such as those of the Elizabethan astrologer Simon Forman and of Samuel Pepys or, closer to our time, Virginia Woolf, intimate memoirs such as Elizabeth Gaskell's *Life of Charlotte Brontë* and documentary films such as we have for some more recent writers – are there, in spite of such absences, ways in which we can attempt to plumb Shakespeare's depths?

To start with, these absences are not total. We have expressions of opinion about him from contemporaries, some

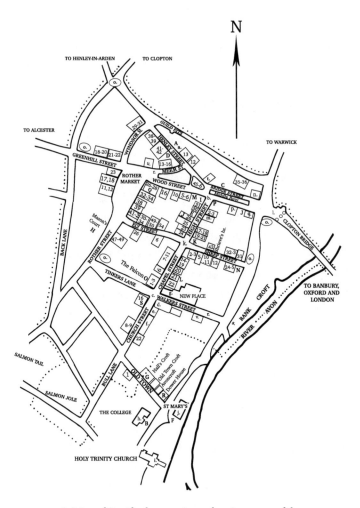

1 Map of Stratford-upon-Avon showing some of the landmarks and buildings present in Shakespeare's time. Stratford had around a thousand elm trees and a population of two thousand people.

Key to map

Some of the buildings that Shakespeare knew and which still survive today

Chapel Street
Nos. 1-3 (now The Falcon from around 1661); 6; 7-11; 14-19; 20 and 21; part of the buildings now known as The Shakespeare (hotel); No 22 (now Nash's House)

Church Street
Nos 8-9; 16; No 22 (now The Windmill)

Ely Street
No. 6 (now The Cross Keys); 26; 30-34; 49-50; 54 (now The Queen's Head)

Greenhill Street
Nos.18-20; 21-22; 23 (now The Old Thatch)

Guild Pits (now Guild Street)
Nos 35-36

Henley Street
No.12 (now the Public Library); 13 (now Hornby Cottage); 29-31; 38-39; 41-42

High Street
Nos. 2-3; 17-18; 19-21; 23-24; 25 (now The Garrick); 26 (now Harvard House); 30-31

Meer Street
Nos. 13-14; 15-16

Old Town
No.1; Old Town Croft; The Dower House; Avoncroft; Hall's Croft

Rother Street
Nos.11-12; 17-18; 34; 38-39; 40-41 (now The Lamplighter); 47-49; Mason's Court

Sheep Street
Shrieve's House; Nos. 2-3; 5; 10-12; 24-25; 31-33; 42

Wood Street
Nos. 5-6; 10; 16; 26-28; 45-46

Location of some of Shakespeare's neighbours at different times of his life

A. George Badger (next door to the Shakespeares)
B. The Combe family (The College)
C. Richard Field (28 Bridge Street)
D. William Greenaway (now 46-49 Henley Street)
E. William Walker (29 High Street)
F. Thomas Greene (St Mary's)
G. John and Susanna Hall (Hall's Croft)
H. Alderman John Gibbs (Mason's Court)
I. Adrian Quiney (31 High Street)
J. Thomas Rogers (26 High Street, Harvard House, and 27-28 High Street)
K. Hamnet and Judith Sadler (22 High Street)
L. July Shaw (21 Chapel Street)
M. Abraham Sturley (5-6 Wood Street)
N. Richard Tyler (now around 23-26 Sheep Street)
O. William Walford (now The Falcon)
P. Thomas and Judith Quiney (1 High Street)
Q. Alderman William Parsons (26-28 Wood Street)
R. William Reynolds (The Dower House)
S. John Sadler (16 Church Street)

Landmarks

a. The Shakespeares' home on Henley Street
b. High Cross or Market Cross (and from 1614 a whipping post)
c. White Cross
d. Guild Chapel
e. School and Guild Hall
f. Almshouses
g. New Place and grounds
h. The College
i. Holy Trinity Church
j. St Mary's
k. Corn Market
l. Toll Gate
m. The town's first recorded jail (5 High Street)
n. The Swan Inn
o. Muck heaps
p. The Crown Inn
q. The Bear Inn
r. Streams
s. The Walkers' Mill
t. The Angel Inn
u. The King House or Hall (now the White Swan)
v. Rowington Cottage
. . . Borough border

posthumous, many of which are gathered together in the two-volume *Shakspere Allusion Book* (badly out of date though that work is – it was published in 1932). These start in 1592, when he was twenty-eight, with the description of him in *Greene's Groatsworth of Wit* as an 'upstart crow'. This is an obviously malicious and envious gibe, and it was rapidly countered by the prolific but congenitally impecunious writer Henry Chettle in his *Kind Heart's Dream*: 'I am as sorry', wrote Chettle, 'as if the original fault had been my fault because myself have seen his [i.e. Shakespeare's] demeanour no less civil than he [is] excellent in the quality he professes, besides divers of worship have reported his uprightness of dealing, which argues his honesty, and his facetious grace in writing, that approves his art.' (This is the first time the word 'facetious', from the Latin meaning 'witty', appears in English; here the phrase 'facetious grace' seems to mean something like 'amusing skill'.) It would be good to know who the 'divers of worship' were. Might they have included Henry Wriothesley, Earl of Southampton, to whom Shakespeare was to dedicate *Venus and Adonis* and *The Rape of Lucrece* in the two following years? Anyhow this is a powerful character reference; and to the best of my belief, the 'upstart crow' jibe is the only denigratory surviving reference to Shakespeare's character made by any of his contemporaries throughout his career.

People liked and admired him. The minor poet John Weever addressed him as 'Honey-tongued Shakespeare' in a poem published in 1599. And he is mentioned favourably in several commendatory poems and in the three anonymously written *Parnassus* plays performed at St John's College, Cambridge around the turn of the century – 'O sweet Master Shakespeare, I'll have his picture in my study at the court', says

Gullio, seeing him as a kind of pin-up boy. His friends and colleagues John Heminges and Henry Condell, in their dedication to the Folio of 1623, also write of his personality. He was their 'worthy friend and fellow whose reputation they wish to keep alive'. And in their preface addressed to 'the great variety of readers', they write of him as a 'gentle expresser of nature'. Of course they are not writing on oath. But the amount of effort that Heminges and Condell, actors by profession and amateurs in the art of editing, must have put into compiling the volume is itself a testimony to their affection for the man who left money for them – along with Richard Burbage, who had died before the Folio went to press – to buy mourning rings.

There are predictably laudatory posthumous comments and tributes in the First Folio, including Ben Jonson's great elegy headed 'To the memory of my beloved the author Mr William Shakespeare and what he hath left us', though this is more concerned with Shakespeare's artistry and his fame than with his personality, but the famously outspoken Jonson does refer to Shakespeare as his 'beloved', says that the 'race / Of Shakespeare's mind and manners brightly shines / In his well-turnèd and true-filèd lines', and calls him 'Sweet' – that word again – 'swan of Avon'.

Ben Jonson also gives us the most intimate surviving testaments to Shakespeare's character in his notebooks published posthumously as *Timber: or Discourses upon men and matter as they have flowed out of his daily readings or had their reflux from his peculiar notion of the times* (1641). These give us what must surely be the most honest and fullest assessment of Shakespeare's character deriving from a contemporary. Jonson says:

I loved the man, and do honour his memory on this side idolatry as much as any. He was indeed honest, and of an open and free nature; had an excellent fancy, brave notions, and gentle expressions, wherein he flowed with that facility that sometime it was necessary he should be stopped. *'Sufflaminandus erat,'* [that is to say, he needed to be checked, or reined in] as Augustus said of Haterius. His wit was in his own power: would the rule of it had been so too. But he redeemed his vices with his virtues. ['Vices' here surely refers to stylistic faults rather than to moral qualities.] There was ever more in him to be praised than to be pardoned.

Jonson's comments on Shakespeare's artistry are interesting but not entirely clear. 'Excellent fancy' presumably means 'a fine imagination'. I suppose 'brave notions, and gentle expressions' means something like 'excellent ideas which he expressed admirably'. Haterius was a Roman orator, presumably inclined to verbosity. In spite of the cautious qualification in 'this side idolatry', Jonson's view that Shakespeare was 'honest, and of an open and free nature' represents a noble and generous character reference from a writer who had once been a professional rival, and moreover it corroborates what Henry Chettle had written many years earlier of the young Shakespeare. Jonson's criticism that Shakespeare sometimes overwrote is one that Shakespeare himself might well have agreed with, judging by both the varying lengths of his plays and by the cuts he or his company made in, for example, the Folio versions of *Richard II* and *Hamlet*.

To the somewhat generalized tributes to Shakespeare's character – his 'uprightness of dealing' – we can add his capacity to keep out of trouble with the law. Most of his fellow playwrights, unlike him, spent time in prison for a variety of offences – Marlowe for, among other crimes, suspected murder; Jonson for killing a man in a duel; Dekker on numerous occasions for debt. Shakespeare seems to have had only two brushes with the law. In 1596 one William Waite served on him and on several other theatre people a writ requiring them to keep the peace 'for fear of death and mutilation of limbs'; according to Schoenbaum, this is 'a conventional legal phrase in such documents'. In other words, this need imply no more than that he took part in an overly boisterous night out with his theatrical friends. The second (which includes a third) brush with the law names him as having defaulted on tax payments in both September 1597 and October 1598. There are no records of prosecutions. Shakespeare on those two occasions was probably simply living away from Bishopsgate – possibly in Stratford-upon-Avon, moving into New Place, and overseeing its renovations. These instances apart, Shakespeare appears to have been exceptionally law-abiding.

What about Shakespeare's outward appearance? And if we knew what he looked like, how much would that tell us about his character? As Viola says in *Twelfth Night*, 'nature with a beauteous wall / Doth oft close in pollution' (1.2.44–45), and, to quote Duncan in *Macbeth*, 'There's no art / To find the mind's construction in the face' (1.4.11–12). Still, we keep on hoping. The popularity of portrait painting in Shakespeare's own time and later, and also, more recently, of photographic portraiture suggests an abiding hope that character may be revealed by outward appearance. We have evidence of varying degrees of reliability about what Shakespeare looked like.

Most reliable, I suppose, are the Droeshout engraving in the First Folio, printed in 1623, certified as a true likeness by Ben Jonson in verses printed below it, and the bust in Holy Trinity Church. It has been generally assumed that the bust was made after his death, but Lena Orlin, in her book *The Private Life of William Shakespeare* (2021), fascinatingly suggests that Shakespeare designed and commissioned it himself. There are also the Chandos and Cobbe portraits, both with claims of good provenance, and the late seventeenth-century report by John Aubrey that he was 'a handsome, well-shaped man'. Some contemporary writers had distinctive features. The satirist Thomas Nashe described Robert Greene's hair as 'A jolly long red peak – like the spire of a steeple' which 'he cherished continually without cutting, whereat a man might hang a jewel, it was so sharp and pendant'. Nashe himself was famous for his unruly shock of hair and his beardlessness – unusual at the time. And Ben Jonson was exceptionally large – he is said to have weighed over twenty stone at one stage of his life, and himself wrote of his 'mountain belly'. Everything suggests, on the other hand, that there was nothing especially striking about Shakespeare's appearance. By contrast with such figures as Marlowe, Nashe, Greene, and Dekker, the figure that the mature Shakespeare cut in public was conventional, middle class – we might even say, respectable. He went to the barber's regularly, both in Stratford and in London, to have his hair cut and his beard neatly trimmed. And there is reason to believe that he – like most gentlemen of the age – wore a signet ring, which would serve both as a personal adornment and for sealing documents, and that it has survived.

2 The memorial demi-figure of Shakespeare in Holy Trinity Church, Stratford-upon-Avon. Unusually, this photograph looks directly into Shakespeare's eyes, and you can see Shakespeare's teeth. The memorial, possibly commissioned by Shakespeare himself, seems at its most expressive from this angle, almost as though Shakespeare were about to speak.

It's a curious story. In 1810 a Mrs Martin was working in a field close to the Stratford churchyard when she turned up a gold ring, almost black with age. It bore the initials 'W. S.' separated by a lover's knot. She took it to a local silversmith, who put it in an acid bath to check the metal, thus restoring its original colour. Of course 'W. S.' does not necessarily stand for 'William Shakespeare', but the local historian Robert Bell Wheler wrote in 1814 that he could find 'no Stratfordian of that period so likely to own such a ring as Shakespeare'. He also intriguingly noted that no seal is affixed to Shakespeare's will, but that 'where the scrivener had

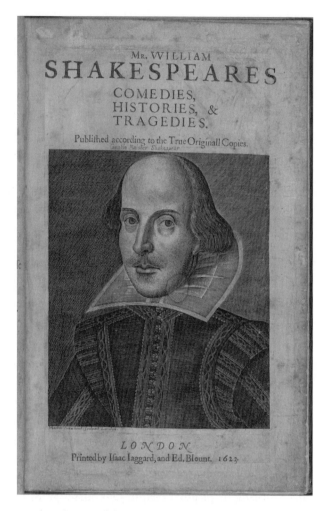

3 The title page of the First Folio advertises the range of Shakespeare's work. The engraved portrait by Martin Droeshout shows a formally costumed Shakespeare in a late stage of baldness. Accompanying verses by Ben Jonson certify it as a good likeness.

written "in witness whereof I have hereunto set my hand and seal" the words "and seal" were struck out, as if Shakespeare had recently lost his seal ring'. Wheler later bought the ring and gave it to his sister, who presented it to the Shakespeare Birthplace Trust in 1868. (Plausible though the story is, it has to be admitted that Shakespeare is not wearing a ring in the only surviving image to show his hands, the memorial bust.)

Various other potentially revealing areas of investigation exist. It is possible, for example, to assess Shakespeare's attitudes to work. We may deduce something about his ambition, his conscientiousness, his industry, by looking at the tasks he undertook. Early in his career he wrote the two long narrative poems *Venus and Adonis* and *The Rape of Lucrece*, published in 1593 and 1594 respectively. Maybe this is because he saw the need for an alternative career while the theatres were closed during outbreaks of plague. In his early years, at least, he worked as an actor – the 1616 Folio of his rival Ben Jonson's plays names him in the actor list of his comedy *Every Man in His Humour*, played at the Curtain in 1598, and as one of the 'principal tragedians' in Jonson's *Sejanus* in 1603, and he heads the list of actors in the 1623 First Folio of his own plays; but 'Less for making' is scribbled beside his name in a copy in the Glasgow University Library, which may suggest that as time passed his colleagues gave him time off from his acting duties so that he could 'make', or write, plays. He worked too as a theatre administrator, helping for two decades to manage a single theatre company, which suggests a high degree of business acumen, of stability of character, and of conscientiousness. Above all he worked as a playwright, producing an average of around two plays a year over two

17

4 Shakespeare's signet ring. This gold signet ring used for sealing documents bearing Shakespeare's initials turned up in a field near Holy Trinity Church in 1810.

decades or more, but ceasing it would seem around 1613, three years before he died. And, as I shall discuss in the next chapter, much serious reading and fundamental brainwork lie behind his writings. He was a hard-working man for most of his life. He was also a man who developed. More clearly, it seems to me, than any other writer of his time, he went on changing, maturing, growing in technical skill and in emotional maturity throughout his career. To read through his complete works in chronological succession is to marvel at their variety, their experimentalism, their emotional range. It is a far cry from *The Two Gentlemen of Verona* to *The Tempest*, from *Titus Andronicus* to *King Lear*, from *King John* to *Coriolanus*. Each work is, to use T. S. Eliot's words, 'a fresh raid on the inarticulate', evidence at one and the same time of an awareness of the commercial value to his company of a varied repertoire but, more inwardly, of an ever-deepening imaginative response to experience.

We may learn more about him too by thinking about how he got on with his theatrical colleagues, observing for instance that they stuck together over long periods of time and that he received a bequest from one of them and made bequests to others. He was a true company man, writing with individual actors in mind for specific roles. He knew his colleagues' strengths and their limitations. As Richard Burbage, his leading actor and co-founder of the Lord Chamberlain's Men, grew older so Shakespeare provided for him star roles that did not require him to appear youthful. It would be interesting to know how long Burbage, born in 1567, went on playing Romeo, written for him when he was about twenty-seven, and Hamlet, the role he created at the age of about thirty-three; certainly the central characters in plays written later in the careers of the playwright and his leading actor are less youthful than in the earlier plays. And in the speech prefixes in the first printed text of *Much Ado About Nothing*, the quarto of 1600, the names of the great comic actor Will Kemp and his colleague Abraham Cowley are printed instead of the names of the characters Dogberry and Verges, suggesting that Shakespeare had these actors in mind as he wrote.

We can learn about Shakespeare too by thinking about his financial affairs, his purchases, and his investments – how extensive they were, where they were, and when and to what end he made them. It is surely significant that he appears to have lived relatively modestly in more than one neighbourhood in London and to have poured

5 Richard Burbage (1568–1619). Member of a theatrical family closely associated with Shakespeare throughout his career, Burbage created most of Shakespeare's leading tragic roles and was deeply mourned on his death.

most of his financial resources into property and land in his hometown. From the age of thirty-three – only three years after the founding of the Lord Chamberlain's Men – he owned New Place, the largest house in the borough of

Stratford-upon-Avon. Five years after this, in 1602, he paid £320 for the Welcombe estate, a property of some 107 acres – almost as big as the whole of the borough of Stratford-upon-Avon (109 acres). And only three years later, in 1605, he paid £440 for a share in the Stratford tithes. His last known investment, and his only known purchase of property in London, came in March 1613 – three months before the destruction by fire of the Globe playhouse – when he, along with three associates, agreed to pay £140 for the lease of the Blackfriars Gatehouse, which was close to the Blackfriars playhouse. Such information may help us to assess where his priorities lay, how much he cared about his family and about his social status.

We can think too about his family concerns. We can examine his will, made not long before he died, and we can think about what it reveals about his standing in the local community at the time of his death, what it suggests about his attitudes to his surviving relatives and friends, to his fellow Stratfordians, and to his theatrical colleagues. But the motives for individual bequests can only be guessed at, and wills were primarily legal documents, not personal testaments. Lena Orlin discusses the interlined bequest to Anne of the second-best bed in exhaustive detail, suggesting finally that it may refer to 'a bed in which Anne may have given birth to three children and from which one of them, some eleven years later, was taken to his grave' (*The Private Life of William Shakespeare*, Oxford University Press, 2021, p. 195).

Even without the aid of psychoanalytical techniques, such as those deployed by Norman Holland and his

6 An artist's reconstruction of New Place. Shakespeare bought this, the biggest house in the borough, in 1597. Archaeological excavations from 2011 to 2016 revealed its full extent. It is thought to have had between twenty and thirty rooms.

associates, we can assess much from Shakespeare's writings about his mental qualities. We can say confidently that he was highly articulate, at least on the page; that he had a wide, flexible vocabulary which developed over the years. We can observe that the Latin that he learnt at school lies on the surface in his earlier writings but goes underground later. We can examine his vocabulary to see what it can tell us about his areas of knowledge such as the law, the court, and the countryside, hunting, shooting and fishing, his familiarity with dialects and with languages other than English, and with various kinds of technical language. We can see how he deployed his vocabulary in his writings, his awareness of rhetorical devices and the development of his skill in using them, his innovative powers. We can observe, for example, that he uses highly specialized language of horse breeding in a speech by Biondello in *The Taming of the Shrew* (3.2.42–61), and that a speech in *Much Ado About Nothing* shows remarkable familiarity with women's clothing – the Duchess of Milan's gown was made of 'cloth o' gold, and cuts, and laced with silver, set with pearls, down sleeves, side sleeves, and skirts round underborne with a bluish tinsel' (3.4.18–21) – and we may wonder where he got all this from.

He clearly had an exceptional sense of verbal rhythm, an ear for the musical qualities of language, and a capacity to tussle with complex ideas. And we know that he was capable of extreme sexual wordplay, used sometimes to scintillatingly comic ends but also in profound explorations of sexual torment and disgust in plays such as *Timon of Athens* and *Troilus and Cressida*, and in the Sonnets.

We have no record of his exercising his verbal skills in private life. Indeed the records of what he actually said are sparse. There is one salacious anecdote, reported in the diary of John Manningham, a lawyer at the Middle Temple, who saw *Twelfth Night* performed there on 2 February 1602. A few weeks later, on 13 March, Manningham wrote:

> Upon a time when Burbage played Richard III there was a citizen grew so far in liking with him that before she went from the play she appointed him to come to her that night by the name of Richard III. Shakespeare, overhearing their conclusion, went before, was entertained and at his

> game ere Burbage came. Then message being brought that
> Richard III was at the door, Shakespeare caused return to
> be made that William the Conqueror was before Richard.

It is a good story, worthy of theatrical circles, and it may be
true. It is funny but of course it has serious biographical implications in its presentation of a promiscuously adulterous
Shakespeare.

The only other contemporary record of words actually spoken by Shakespeare is of an occasion on which he said
very little. In the spring of 1612 he was called upon to give
evidence in a London lawsuit involving the family of Christopher Mountjoy, a French Huguenot immigrant whose wife,
Marie, manufactured elaborate headdresses for court ladies
(and perhaps also for actors.) Shakespeare had acted as go-be-
tween in marriage negotiations between their daughter, Mary,
and Mountjoy's apprentice, Stephen Belott. He may even have
supervised a hand-fasting agreement between them such as
he portrays taking place between Orlando and Rosalind in
As You Like It (Act 4, Scene 1, 116–189). His memory of what
happened is imperfect and the evidence he gave is reported in
legal language, but the case shows him in a favourable light as
helping a pair of young lovers in their marriage negotiations.

The sparse records of conversations and correspond-
ence with his Stratford friends about the controversial Welcombe enclosures tell us little, though Duncan-Jones may be
right in discerning a significant, even hypocritical division
between the man who can make King Lear pray for 'poor
homeless wretches' and the landowner who, a few years after writing that, seems more concerned about his financial
security than about the interests of the poor people of his

native town. People don't always practise what they preach, and Shakespeare was clearly interested in securing what was best for his family.

We can deduce much from Shakespeare's writings about his education, and we can relate this to what is known of the curriculum of the school that was available to him. Sometimes, especially in his early plays, he quotes directly from works of classical literature in the original language (repeatedly, for example, in *Titus Andronicus*). We know a lot about the amount of reading he had to do for some, at least, of his plays. We can assess his knowledge of the Bible, and we may try to deduce which parts of it he found most to his taste. We can even deduce what he was reading at certain times. To give one example, in *Antony and Cleopatra* Mark Antony's 'Then must thou needs find out new heaven, new earth' echoes the Book of Revelation, 21: 1. (Naseeb Shaheen in *Biblical References in Shakespeare's Plays* (University of Delaware Press, 1992) says that 'Shakespeare's use of the Bible in *Antony and Cleopatra* is outstanding' (p. 644).) We can argue, as people have interminably argued, about whether his writings betray his religious leanings – Was he a Protestant? Did he have Roman Catholic sympathies? How did he feel both personally and professionally about Puritanism? If I had to express my own views I should say that he was a conforming Protestant, did not have Roman Catholic sympathies, and profoundly disliked the Puritans.

We can see, from the sources that he drew upon, that he went on reading assiduously and widely throughout his working life, and we may make deductions from this about his sociability – aided perhaps by John Aubrey's remark, dating admittedly from late in the seventeenth century, that he 'was not a company keeper; lived in Shoreditch; wouldn't be debauched, and, if invited to, writ he was in pain'. He needed time to himself. We can see that he had a taste for, or at least that he saw that he could make use in his own work of, certain sorts of literature – the poetry of his contemporaries and predecessors such as Geoffrey Chaucer, Christopher Marlowe, and Sir Philip Sidney; works of English and classical history; Italianate romance; popular English fiction by writers including Robert Greene and Thomas Lodge; philosophical writings including the essays of Montaigne; studies of contemporary issues such as *A Declaration of Egregious Popish Impostures* by Samuel Harsnett (1603) (Harsnett became Archbishop of York), which influenced *King Lear* – and we can be certain from the date of publication of some of these books that he remained an assiduous reader for most, at least, of his life. We may note absences from the record, too, such as the small impact on his work of Edmund Spenser's *Faerie Queene* (1590).

We can envisage Shakespeare as both a playgoer and a reader of dramatic and poetic texts, interacting with contemporary literary and dramatic trends, following some and ignoring others, and we can think what, if anything, this tells us about his personal cast of mind. We can deduce that he saw and learnt from plays and poems written by his contemporaries, including Marlowe, whose poem *Hero and Leander* clearly influenced *Venus and Adonis* and who is the only contemporary to whom, under the guise of a 'dead shepherd' (*As You Like It*, 3.5.82), he alludes in his plays, as well as writers such as Thomas Kyd, Thomas Nashe, Richard Barnfield, Samuel Daniel, and of course Ben Jonson.

26

Still developing studies in authorship and dramatic collaboration suggest that in his earlier years Shakespeare was enough of a team player to collaborate with George Peele (on *Titus Andronicus*), and possibly with Thomas Nashe and Christopher Marlowe. From the founding of the Lord Chamberlain's Men in 1594 onwards we can see him continuing to plough his own furrow as an essentially romantic dramatist in the face of the growing popularity of city comedy, led by Ben Jonson, and of satirical tragedy in the works of writers such as John Marston and Thomas Middleton, even though in his later years he found enough sympathy with Middleton to collaborate with him and to draw on his individual talents for the more satirical scenes of *Timon of Athens*; and we can perhaps more readily understand how he found a congenial collaborator in the romantically inclined John Fletcher (1579–1625), a younger man who may have seen Shakespeare as a mentor. At the same time we may wonder how he got on in his collaboration on *Pericles* with the villainous George Wilkins, brothel keeper and woman beater; indeed, our knowledge that he worked with Wilkins may extend our sense of his powers of social adaptability.

Through study of texts on which Shakespeare collaborated with other writers we can think about what collaboration involved. It doesn't for example necessarily mean that he sat down in the same room as Marlowe or Middleton or Fletcher or Wilkins, and that they worked on both plot and dialogue in intimate communion. Ben Jonson boasts in the Prologue to *Volpone* that he wrote the play single-handed within the space of five weeks:

'Tis known, five weeks fully penned it
From his own hand, without a coadjutor,
Novice, journeyman, or tutor.

Here Jonson usefully identifies four different kinds of collaborator. 'Coadjutor' is an ecclesiastical term referring to a bishop's assistant, so here I suppose we may take it to apply to a more or less equal collaborator; 'novice' seems to imply a beginner or apprentice playwright, 'journeyman' a hack writer, and 'tutor' an experienced writer working alongside and advising a novice. George Peele, with whom it is now believed Shakespeare worked on the early *Titus Andronicus*, was eight years older than Shakespeare. Was he, as it were, the tutor and Shakespeare the novice? If Shakespeare really did collaborate with his almost exact contemporary Christopher Marlowe, were they genuine coadjutors or was the already more experienced Marlowe in charge? Or did they perhaps devise plots together and then write their allotted scenes independently? In Shakespeare's later years, was he perhaps 'tutor' to Thomas Middleton and John Fletcher, both of whom were about sixteen years younger than he?

Study of the structure of his plays can help us to identify qualities of mind that made him successful as a plotter, as someone who could construct a complex dramatic structure, who had a practical knowledge of the theatrical conditions of his time, of the limitations imposed by the fact that only male actors would appear in his plays, that he needed to lay out his plot so that an individual actor might be required to take more than one role. We can sometimes identify limitations in his dramatic technique, and developments in it as he gained in experience. Even early in his career there is a great leap forward between the relatively amateurish plotting of *The Two Gentlemen of Verona* – which I believe to be his first play – and the masterly construction of *The Comedy of Errors*, written only a few years later, in 1594.

We can see him as an observer of the life around him, as someone who knew, whether from direct experience or through his reading, about domestic life, about the law, and music, and philosophy, about plants and gardens, and about hunting and wildlife. We can think – as I shall do in the last chapter – about his sense of humour, what made him laugh – or at least what he thought might make other people laugh. We can think about his sense of individual character, both by observing how he makes characters in his plays speak and behave and also by observing what he makes them say about other characters in their plays, their moral attitudes, their foibles and sensitivities. We can look at his portrayal of human idiosyncrasy, observing his sympathetic amusement at the ramblings of the Nurse in *Romeo and Juliet* and of Justice Shallow in *Henry IV, Part Two*, at the immature illusions of the lords in *Love's Labour's Lost*, the affected language of Osric in *Hamlet*, the social pretensions of the Old Shepherd and his son in *The Winter's Tale*. We can try to assess his sensibility by examining how in his plays he imagines himself into his characters' attitudes to the life around them. We can observe, for example, that he was capable of empathizing with the suffering of animals: 'the poor beetle that we tread upon / In corporal sufferance finds a pang as great / As when a giant dies,' says Isabella in *Measure for Measure* (3.1.77–79). And in *Pericles* Marina evinces the same kind of sensibility:

> Believe me, la.
> I never killed a mouse nor hurt a fly.
> I trod once on a worm against my will,
> But I wept for it.   (Scene 15, 126–129)

We can wonder how common such empathy was at the time – I remember my mentor Professor Terence Spencer saying that he had observed it only in Shakespeare and Montaigne.

Reverting to the life records, we can think about Shakespeare's dedications to the young Earl of Southampton, nine and a half years his junior, of his narrative poems, *Venus and Adonis* (1593) and *The Rape of Lucrece* (1594) – the second expressed in unconventionally loving terms – and what they may imply about his relationship with the Earl, and we can link this with related anecdotal evidence, such as the legend that Southampton gave him a thousand pounds (it seems an awful lot, but the *Oxford English Dictionary* allows that the word 'thousand' had for several centuries been 'used vaguely or hyperbolically for a large number', so it may just have been a way of saying that the Earl gave him a hell of a lot of money. 'I owe you a thousand pound,' says Falstaff to Justice Shallow (*2 Henry IV*, 5.5.73)). In contrast to this is Shakespeare's apparent lack of concern for the publication of his plays. Is it because publication would have brought him little or no money? Or because he was indifferent to the opinions of the reading public? Or simply that he was too busy? Was his bequest of money to Heminges and Condell and Burbage motivated by the hope that they would publish the 1623 Folio? And we may ask how his attitude to publication compares with that of contemporary playwrights.

7 Henry Wriothesley, Earl of Southampton, as a young man.
This oil painting of the Earl aged around nineteen was believed
to depict a woman until the late twentieth century. He was
proud of his long tresses, depicted in other portraits.

We can think about the absences in the literary as
well as the biographical record; about for instance the fact
that in spite of his massive literary talent he wrote almost
entirely for the theatre, taking little or no interest in the
printing of his plays, that he appears not to have written
masques for the court, or pageants for the City, or what we
may call 'public' poems such as commendatory verses for
other writers' work, or comments on national events, or
tributes on the death of members of the royal family such

as Queen Elizabeth in 1603 or the young Prince Henry in 1612 – both of which elicited extensive comment from fellow writers. We can wonder about his mystical poem 'The Phoenix and the Turtle' of 1601 – How did it come to be published? What are its apparently esoteric significances? What relationship, if any, did Shakespeare have to Sir John Salusbury, who was associated with the volume in which the poem appeared and whose son addressed a sonnet to his 'good friends' Heminges and Condell on the publication of the 1623 Folio, saying that they had 'pleased the living, loved the dead'?

If there's anywhere that Shakespeare seems to be speaking in his own person it is in his sonnets. How personal are they? To what extent, if at all, are they based on real-life situations in which he was implicated? How much do they reveal about his relationships with other men and with women? Were they written for love or for money? Were they intended for publication? Are they truly a sonnet sequence, intended to be read from start to finish? The sonnets are so central to the theme of this book that I shall devote the whole of the third chapter to them.

We can think about the implications for Shakespeare's personality of his choice of subject matter for his plays, of the fact that almost all of them are set in the past and (except of course for the English history plays) in foreign lands. And in relation to this we can consider how his choice of subject matter compares with that of his contemporaries – of his fondness for Italian sources, of the comparative absence from his plays of clear topical reference, of his general avoidance of direct contemporary satire.

We can observe his sympathetic portrayal of morally dubious characters such as Bardolph and Doll Tearsheet (in *Henry IV, Part Two*), Paroles (in *All's Well That Ends Well*), Sir Toby Belch (in *Twelfth Night*), and even Falstaff (in *Henry IV, Parts One* and *Two*, and *The Merry Wives of Windsor*), and we can contrast this with his evident dislike of such cold fish as Prince John (in *Henry IV, Part Two*), and Angelo (in *Measure for Measure*), Don John (in *Much Ado About Nothing*), Octavius Caesar (in *Antony and Cleopatra*), or Giacomo (in *Cymbeline*). Some characters in his plays, such as Richard III and Iago, may seem unmitigatedly evil, but other villains, such as Macbeth and even Edmund (in *King Lear*), are portrayed with some degree of sympathy and understanding, and he is not judgemental about, for example, the illicit passions of Antony and Cleopatra.

We can, I think, deduce something about Shakespeare's personal opinions from the plays. He seems to me to have distrusted people, like Iago in *Othello*, and Goneril, Regan, and above all Edmund, in *King Lear*, who express a severely rationalistic view of life and of morality, and to have sympathized more easily with the sceptical irrationality of Edmund's father, Gloucester and indeed of Hamlet. There is a speech by Lafeu in *All's Well That Ends Well*, unnecessary to the action, in which I think that for once we can hear Shakespeare speaking: 'They say miracles are past, and we have our philosophical persons to make modern [meaning 'commonplace'] and familiar things [that are] supernatural and causeless. Hence is it that we make trifles of terrors, ensconcing ourselves into seeming knowledge when we should submit ourselves to an unknown fear'

(2.3.1–6). He is suggesting that 'clever', excessively rational people, try to reduce to a commonplace level matters that are beyond human understanding, reducing the mysteries of the universe to a series of scientific formulae, making 'trifles of terrors' instead of opening their imaginations to the fullness of experience – or, as he puts it, submitting themselves 'to an unknown fear'– that is, to the uncertainties of the unknown and unknowable. It is an exact description of the error that Lady Macbeth makes in thinking that she can ignore the promptings of the imagination. 'Make thick my blood,' she says as she prepares to urge her husband to murder Duncan, 'Stop up th'access and passage to remorse, / That no compunctious visitings of nature / Shake my fell purpose' (*Macbeth*, 1.5.43–45). Essentially, it seems to me, this identifies Shakespeare as someone who acknowledges the mystery of human life but is not bound by any dogma.

We can also, I suggest, discern something about the subconscious workings of Shakespeare's mind in images not directly demanded by the narrative, in a manner that was adumbrated by Caroline Spurgeon in her book *Shakespeare's Imagination and What It Tells Us* (1935) and, more subtly, by Edward Armstrong in his *Shakespeare's Imagination: A Study of the Psychology of Association and Inspiration* of 1943, where he discerns recurrent image clusters that help to track the working of Shakespeare's subconscious mind. He shows, for example, that the word 'hum' is closely associated in Shakespeare's mind with death: 'Shakespeare uses the word in twenty contexts and in twelve of these there is death or sleep imagery' (p. 45).

8 Ellen Terry (1847–1928) as Princess Innogen in *Cymbeline*. This miniature showing Innogen imagining Posthumus's departure belonged to Terry's great-nephew, Sir John Gielgud, who kept it on his theatre dressing table.

I notice too a recurrent preoccupation with imagery of diminution, as in Edgar's description of Dover Cliff:

> The fishermen, that walk upon the beach,
> Appear like mice; and yond tall anchoring bark,
> Diminished to her cock; her cock, a buoy
> Almost too small for sight.
>
>   (*The Tragedy of King Lear*, 4.5.17–20)

It comes again elsewhere, as in Innogen's imagining of Posthumus's departure:

> I would have broke mine eye-strings; cracked them, but
> To look upon him, till the diminution

35

> Of space had pointed him sharp as my needle;
> Nay, followed him till he had melted from
> The smallness of a gnat to air, and then
> Have turned mine eye and wept …
>
> (*Cymbeline*, 1.4.17–22)

And maybe this preoccupation relates also to recurrent imagery of a coming together of opposites, as several times in *The Winter's Tale*, as when Camillo says of Leontes and Polixenes

> … they have seemed to be together, though absent;
> shook hands, as over a vast; and embraced as it were
> from the ends of opposed winds   (1.1.28–31)

and in the Clown's

> I am not to say it is a sea, for it is now the sky. Betwixt
> the firmament and it you cannot thrust a bodkin's point.
>   (3.3.82–84)

And this observational quality is also present in *Othello*:

> For do but stand upon the foaming shore,
> The chidden billow seems to pelt the clouds,
> The wind-shaked surge with high and monstrous mane
> Seems to cast water on the burning Bear
> And quench the guards of th'ever-fixed Pole.   (2.1.11–15)

These are just a few instances of points in the plays where the poetic content seems to me to be determined as much by Shakespeare's subconscious mind as by his literary intentions.

In brief, it seems to me that Shakespeare lived a life of external respectability and that he achieved personal popularity and worldly success, but the amazing degree of imaginative fecundity and emotional ferment to which his works bear abundant witness surely reflects a life of inner turmoil. His life is a tale of two cities (or one town and one city). In Stratford he is the prosperous and outwardly respectable family man. But he leads a double life, disappearing at frequent intervals to the metropolis. There he is the successful poet, actor, and playwright, leading member of the most successful theatre company of the age, a frequenter of the royal court and also of the Inns of Court. I see him as a man whose inner tensions were contained with stern self-discipline in an external appearance of harmony, but who found release in the creative energy that informs his plays and especially in his Sonnets. In the most intimate of those, I believe, he delved deeply into his innermost being, discovering for himself what manner of man he was and in the process revealing a tortured sexual life. I discuss the Sonnets in the third chapter, but in the next one I shall remain with Shakespeare's professional life and consider how he wrote his plays.

2 *How Did Shakespeare Write a Play?*

 ❧

S HAKESPEARE was both a non-dramatic poet and a playwright. It's not too difficult to understand how he became a poet. The King's New School in Stratford-upon-Avon provided its pupils with a primarily literary education and Shakespeare may have started writing poems when he was still at school. The two sonnets printed last in the collection published in 1609 are translations of a poem originally written by the fifth-century AD Greek poet Marianus Scolasticus and may have been originally written as schoolboy exercises. The sonnet numbered 153 appears to be a revision of No. 154, as if perhaps the schoolmaster had made criticisms of the boy's first shot at it. And it is generally agreed that Sonnet 145, which ends with a pun on the name of Anne Hathaway – "'I hate" from hate away she threw, / And saved my life, saying, "not you'" – is a teenage effusion, a wooing poem written, if not while Shakespeare was still at school, at any rate not long after he left. This is only the first of the many puns which, for better or for worse, trickled – sometimes flooded – from his pen.

During his schooldays, too, he could have started to develop an interest in drama. His father invited the first troupes of professional players to perform in Stratford in the year he led the Corporation as Bailiff. Shakespeare was four years old. Plays by classical dramatists, such as Terence and Plautus, were probably on the school curriculum – and Plautus was to give him plot material for one of his early plays, *The Comedy of Errors,* performed in 1594. In 1583, when Shakespeare was nineteen, the town officials subsidized an amateur performance of a play, now lost, organized by one Davy Jones, who later married a member of the Hathaway family. Shakespeare must surely have seen it and may well have been involved, as actor or even as writer. Travelling professional companies performed in the guildhall. During 1586 to 1587, for instance, five companies visited the town. So it's not at all surprising that he should have been stage-struck.

It's not possible, however, to establish how he started his career as a professional playwright. It's all bound up with the so-called 'lost years' – the period of his life between the birth of his twins in 1585 and the reference to him as an 'upstart crow' in *Greene's Groatsworth of Wit* in 1592. We know virtually nothing of him during this time. The most popular and reasonable hypothesis is that at some point he joined a company of players, perhaps while they were on tour, and that sooner or later he gravitated towards London. Recent studies in authorship support the belief that early in his career he, like many others, wrote sometimes in collaboration, perhaps initially in a kind of apprenticeship, with other professional writers including George Peele (on *Titus Andronicus*) and perhaps Christopher Marlowe and Thomas Kyd. His early co-authored plays were presumably offered to or commissioned by theatre managers who may have exerted influence over their content and style. I believe *The Two*

Gentlemen of Verona to be his first solo-authored play, apprentice work possibly drafted even before he left Stratford. Other early plays in which he had at least a main hand include *The Taming of the Shrew*, the highly sophisticated tragedy of *Richard III*, generally dated 1593, and *The Comedy of Errors* – surely solo-authored – performed probably for the first time at Gray's Inn before the lawyers on 28 December 1594.

It was in this year that he became a shareholder on the founding of the Lord Chamberlain's Men. It is the most important milestone in his professional career. For something like a decade after this all his plays are solo-authored. But even during this period he was not in the position of a wholly independent, freelance dramatist. He was a company man, with both artistic and financial responsibilities towards his colleagues, and it seems likely that in deciding on the subject matter and style of his next play he would have consulted his colleagues about their needs. One can imagine company meetings with anxious discussions about box office receipts, the activities of rival companies, the need for plays that would show off the skills of the company's leading actors, playing to their strengths while respecting their limitations, and the search for talented boys to replace those whose voices were breaking.

Shakespeare was constrained too, throughout his career, by legal and social requirements and by governmental censorship. It was, for instance, forbidden from early in the reign of Queen Elizabeth (by an ordinance of 1559) for plays to be written on biblical subjects. And it was dangerous for a dramatist to engage directly with contemporary political issues. Even episodes which, while not being explicitly top-ical, might be interpreted as commenting on current events were sensitive: so for example the episode in *Richard II* relat-ing to the King's abdication was omitted from editions of the play printed before the death, in 1603, of Queen Elizabeth, for whom this was a sensitive issue. Presumably when Shake-speare wrote the play he failed to see how the episode might be interpreted. And from 1606 onwards, with the passing of the 'act to restrain abuses of players', it was forbidden to use profane language, and existing dramatic texts were revised to bring them into conformity with this. The 1622 quarto text of *Othello*, written before the Act was passed – probably in 1603 or 1604 – contains fifty or more profanities that are not pres-ent, or that are toned down, in the Folio text, printed from a censored theatrical manuscript.

Shakespeare would have been conscious too that his company needed plays that would not only please the public audiences at the Globe (from 1599) and on tour but would also go down well at court in performances before the reign-ing monarch to which in theory, at least, all the company's endeavours were directed. We know of some 170 perfor-mances that the Lord Chamberlain's, later the King's, Men gave at court from the company's foundation in 1594 to the time of Shakespeare's death. These were well-rewarded and highly prestigious events, given before members of the roy-al family and their guests, the cream of the aristocracy, and visiting dignitaries such as ambassadors and foreign courti-ers. Shakespeare must have been a familiar figure at the royal court. Some of his plays, such as *The Merry Wives of Wind-sor*, with its celebrations of the Order of the Garter (usually omitted in modern performance), and *Macbeth*, with its egregious flattery of King James I, bear obvious witness to the importance to the company of court patronage. And the wide range of dramatic styles that Shakespeare adopted, the fact that he composed an average of around two plays a year, and that he moved freely among the dramatic genres, all indicate his sensitivity to company demands.

To say this is not to imply that Shakespeare was no more than a hack writer, turning out plays to order. It merely reflects the fact that he needed to balance practical with artistic considerations, that he was able to serve his company while also challenging them, himself, and his audiences by producing plays that were both commercially viable and artistically satisfying. He did not rest on his laurels or repeat a formula that he found successful. But he did respond to popular demand, for example in the Falstaff plays, as we see in the epilogue to *Henry IV, Part Two*: 'If you be not too much cloyed with fat meat, our humble author will continue the story with Sir John in it, and make you merry with fair Catherine of France, where, for anything I know, Falstaff shall die of a sweat – unless already 'a be killed with your hard opinions'. But the tone here is playful. The author is not as humble as he pretends to be – he keeps his options open. And though *The Merry Wives of Windsor* shows that he was aware of the commercial appeal of Falstaff, it is naive to believe that the play is a mere pot-boiler that can legitimately be flattened into a mechanical farce as it often is in productions.

It is a measure equally of Shakespeare's professionalism and of his artistic integrity that each play has its own voice, as becomes especially clear if one reads his plays in the (necessarily partly conjectural) order of composition. In this he differs greatly from, for instance, John Lyly, or even Ben Jonson, whose plays are more restricted in range. And though he knew that he had to please, he was willing, especially as he grew older – more confident of himself, less dependent on popular success – to push the boundaries, sometimes seeming almost to be writing for himself rather than for the populace. *Troilus and Cressida* and *Cymbeline*, for example, are stylistically challenging; we have little evidence as to how these and some other plays fared with contemporary audiences. But it is clear from numerous references to *Hamlet* soon after composition that, for all its exceptional length and intellectual sophistication, it, at least, was well received – which says a lot for the audiences of the time. And *King Lear*, his most uncompromising tragedy, was thought suitable to be acted before the King and his family at court on St Stephen's Day night (26 December, Boxing Day) 1606. Not exactly a pantomime.

How Did Shakespeare Choose His Plots?

Before Shakespeare even started to write a play he had to choose or to invent a story that was suitable for dramatization. Almost all his plays are based to some degree or other on one or more pre-existing narratives, some historical in origin, others fictional, some already in dramatic form. And he consulted some of these stories, especially the historical ones, in multiple versions. *Richard II*, for instance, is indebted not only to Marlowe's play *Edward II*, which he could have seen on stage, but also to printed books including Holinshed's and

Froissart's *Chronicles*, Samuel Daniel's epic poem on the Civil Wars, and *The Mirror for Magistrates*. Sometimes too he would combine more than one storyline within the framework of a single play – *King Lear*, for instance, is based partly on an old play of unknown authorship, acted in 1594 but not printed till 1605, and on other versions of the story of Lear, but in addition Sir Philip Sidney's *Arcadia* provided material for the Gloucester plot and Samuel Harsnet's *Declaration of Egregious Popish Impostures* of 1603 influenced the portrayal of Edgar. All this means that Shakespeare had to do a lot of preliminary spadework before he even began to invent a structure for his play. He needed, and the company must have allowed him, time for reading. I find it irresistible to conjecture that they made it possible for him to move away from his London lodgings from time to time to the relative peace and quiet of a study – which we know existed – in New Place.

Some of the books he had read at school clearly gave him material for both the stories and for details of his plays and poems. Ovid's *Metamorphoses* is a pervasive influence from the early *Titus Andronicus* and the narrative poem *Venus and Adonis*, published in 1593, right through to his last solo-authored play, *The Tempest*, in which he cribs almost wholesale from Ovid for one of Prospero's greatest speeches ('Ye elves of hills …'). The book itself appears on stage in both *Titus Andronicus* and *Cymbeline*. And it is clear that throughout his working life Shakespeare was an assiduous reader – and not only for professional reasons.

He read earlier English writers including Geoffrey Chaucer, whose 'Knight's Tale' contributed to both *A Midsummer Night's Dream* and *The Two Noble Kinsmen*, and John

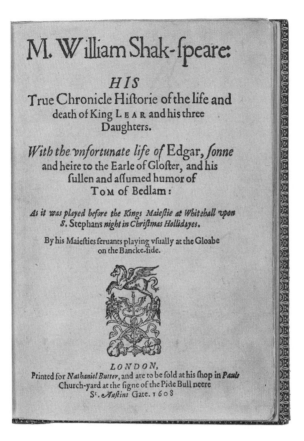

9 Title page to *King Lear*, 1608. The title page to the first edition of *King Lear* offers information about the play's main plot, its subplot, and its first court performance. It had probably been acted at the Globe earlier that year.

Gower (*c.* 1330–1408), author of *Confessio Amantis* (*A Lover's Confession*, *c.* 1386–1390), who appears on stage as the Chorus to *Pericles*; he plundered Arthur Brooke's long poem *Romeus and Juliet*, published in 1562, for his play on the same subject.

He knew John Lyly's immensely popular prose narrative *Euphues* (1586–1588), parodied in *Henry IV, Part One*, as well as plays by Lyly, which helped him to write in the courtly style of his early comedies; he read books about English history, especially Holinshed's *Chronicles* – a vast work which in its longest version, of 1587, runs, it has been computed by Stuart Gillespie, to 'about 3,500,000 words', making it 'roughly equal to the total of the Authorized version of the Bible, the complete dramatic works of Shakespeare, *Clarissa*, Boswell's *Life of Johnson*, and *War and Peace*'. Shakespeare quotes almost verbatim from Holinshed in the (rather boring) opening scene of *Henry V*, but did not necessarily read it from cover to cover.

He read books of classical history too, especially Sir Thomas North's fine translation of Plutarch's *Lives of the Roman and Greek Emperors*, first published in 1579 with expanded editions in 1595 and 1603; he read translations into English of Italian and other romance stories, such as those by Boccaccio, Bandello, and many other writers gathered together by William Painter in the collection *The Palace of Pleasure* (1556; expanded 1567 and 1575), which was to be plundered for plots by many other Elizabethan and Jacobean playwrights and which explains why so many plays of the period are set in Italy.

He read English fiction such as Thomas Lodge's *Rosalynde* (1580), which formed the basis for *As You Like It*, and Robert Greene's *Pandosto* (1588), on which he based the plot and some of the dialogue of *The Winter's Tale*. He appears too to have read Cinthio's *Gli Hecatommithi*, of 1565, which gave him the story for *Othello*, in Italian, and John Eliot's satirically entertaining French conversation manual *Ortho-epia Gallica* of 1593, which is echoed in *Henry V* and in other plays and which he may have bought in order to teach himself French. In *The Merchant of Venice*, Portia mocks her English suitor, Falconbridge, because 'He hath neither Latin, French, nor Italian' (1.2.66–67). I like to think that Shakespeare would not have written this unless he too had been able to understand these languages. All this shows that he was not just a jobbing playwright but a highly cultivated man of letters.

Having chosen the narrative material of a play, Shakespeare had to create a plot, a kind of framework resembling a maquette from which a sculptor might work, or an architect's ground plan, or a scriptwriter's storyboard – a storyline that would give him a structure for his play, deciding how to introduce his narrative material and to establish his characters, how to introduce and to shape any subplot or other material extraneous to the principal narrative that he might find desirable, and how to bring it all to a conclusion. And he had to do all this in ways that would fit the physical structures of the theatres of his time and the strengths and limitations of the acting company at his disposal.

These were tasks that required considerable intellectual effort and which must have occupied his mind and imagination even before he started to compose a play's dialogue. He knew that the theatrical conventions of his time required plays to be of a certain length, though the limits were flexible. It is difficult for us to estimate how long the plays would have lasted in contemporary performance, but the fact that they vary in line length from around 1,800 lines for *The Comedy of Errors* to about 4,000 for *Hamlet* shows that though there may have been minimum expectations there were no fixed limits. Comedies tended to be shorter than tragedies or chronicle history plays. And when we have more than one early text for a particular play, as for example for *A Midsummer Night's Dream* and *Othello*, *Hamlet*, and *King Lear*, their lengths are not identical.

This reflects the fact that Shakespeare may have wished to make changes between first having a manuscript transcribed for his actors and their putting it into production. It also relates to the fact that the text of a play would have been affected by the local conditions under which it was performed. This is illustrated in Act 1, Scene 2 of *A Midsummer Night's Dream*, where we see the players having to write a new prologue to assure the ladies in the court audience that the actors 'will do no harm with their swords'; arguing about its versification; discussing how to modify Lion's appearance so as not to 'fear the ladies'; suggesting that a window of the great chamber where they are to play should be left open to let moonlight in; and discussing how to present a wall: 'You can never bring in a wall!' says Snout (who nevertheless eventually comes on as Wall). This is all exaggerated for comic effect, of course. Still it is interesting that the two surviving texts of the play, the quarto of 1600 which appears to reflect Shakespeare's first thoughts, and the Folio of 1623, which appears to reflect changes made during rehearsal, incorporate significant changes. In the later version, Egeus speaks lines given to Philostrate in the earlier, as if to save an actor. And the speech (5.1.43–60) listing the entertainments to be offered to the Duke for his wedding celebrations is spoken entirely by the Duke in the earlier version; in the later it is divided between him and Lysander, with the Duke commenting on the titles, as if the actor playing the Duke had complained that expecting him both to read the titles and to comment on them was too much like ventriloquism.

These are only two of many examples that could be given to show how some of the early texts reveal the fluidity of play scripts in the period, and the way they would have to be adapted to changing circumstances of performance. Custom-built London theatres had features such as a trapdoor (for Ophelia's grave, for example), an upper level (for Juliet's appearance at a window in what has come, anachronistically, to be called the balcony scene), and flying machinery (for the appearance of Jupiter in *Cymbeline*). But these features were absent in other venues, such as locations provided by the royal court, a great house, or a local guildhall when the players were on tour. Also – like the anonymously written text of 'Pyramus and Thisbe', the play within the play in *A Midsummer Night's Dream* – adaptation might need to be carried out by the actors themselves, or by a 'journeyman' – hack writer – without the original playwright's input. We have reason to believe, for example, that the only text of *Macbeth* that has come down to us is a version by Thomas Middleton made for the King's Men which shortens the original and adds both dialogue and musical elements.

What Dramatic Forms Were Available to Shakespeare?

Shakespeare had dramatic models which he could observe, follow, modify, or reject. He knew about the traditional genres of tragedy and comedy, though he conspicuously refused to be constrained by them throughout his career.

He wrote his plays as continuous structures, flowing smoothly from beginning to end. He knew of the five-act structure favoured by Roman dramatists such as Plautus and Terence, and imitated by some of his English predecessors. *Gammer Gurton's Needle*, for instance, written around 1566 (probably by one William Stevenson), is a robust English comedy which nevertheless follows the neoclassical unities of place, action, and time. But he refused to be bound by the practice of his predecessors. Understanding of the freedom with which he handled dramatic structure has been undermined by the fact that the compilers of the First Folio, along with later editors, imposed on the plays a division into five acts, each broken up into separate scenes, which is foreign to his method of dramatic composition. In general the plays printed in his lifetime are un-divided into acts and scenes, and this appears to reflect the way they were performed at least until 1609, when the King's Men began to make use of the indoor Blackfriars playhouse; there the practicalities of, for instance, trimming the candles used to illuminate the playhouse favoured the observance of act breaks. Moreover, the company employed a highly accomplished band of musicians who performed both before and during the intervals of the action as well as providing, for instance, fanfares for the entrance of royal characters, sound effects for battle scenes, and music for dances, and whose members appeared on stage as in the touching episode in *Romeo and Juliet* (4.4.59 to end) in which musicians who have come to celebrate Juliet's wedding remain to mourn her death.

Sadly, little of the music composed for these purposes – or indeed for the plays in general – has survived. The printed texts contain music cues, but I suspect that they give an inadequate impression of the amount of music that would have been played in early performance.

Shakespeare and Dramatic Genre

Shakespeare's plays are generically mixed. Although he knew, of course, of the 'pure' comedies of earlier dramatists including some written in English as well as in Latin, and also of unmixed tragedies such as those of the Roman dramatist Seneca, which had been published in English translation in 1581, and which had influenced some of his immediate predecessors, he rebelled against their conventions. Here again the compilers of the First Folio have been misleading. On their title page and in the body of the book they divided the plays into three dramatic categories – comedies, histories, and tragedies – misleadingly, since whereas the terms 'comedy' and 'tragedy' refer to the form of plays, 'histories' refers to their content. Some of Shakespeare's plays based on English history, such as *Richard II* and *Richard III*, approximate to tragedy in form insofar as they end with the death of a central character, whereas others, such as *Henry IV, Parts One* and *Two*, which have Falstaff as a central character, are closer to comedies; and indeed *Henry V* ends, like many comedies of the period, with the marriage of its hero as well as with his victory in battle.

The Act of Composition

How, then, may we imagine Shakespeare, once he had agreed with his colleagues what sort of a play was needed, and having chosen a story to dramatize, setting about the task of actually writing it, and what kinds of intellectual, imaginative, and practical qualities would the task have required?

As ideas formed in his mind he might have started to make a note of opportunities that the narrative material afforded for especially effective moments of action – the appearance of a ghost, a sleepwalking scene, a play within the play, a climactic battle; to jot down ideas for characters – a comic nurse, an affected courtier, a bumbling local official, a mischievous fairy. And some speeches in his plays have a self-contained quality which suggests that he might even have roughed them out in advance of writing the body of the play – think for example of Theseus's speech on imagination, 'The lunatic, the lover and the poet / Are of imagination all compact ...' (*A Midsummer Night's Dream* from 5.1.7), or Hamlet's 'To be or not to be' (3.1.59–90), or Prospero's 'Ye elves of hills, brooks, standing lakes and groves' (*The Tempest*, 5.1.33–57) – before he plotted the play's action. Most importantly, he would have to think about how his narrative material related to conventions of dramatic form and to expectations of genre, whether he could best relate it to conventions of comedy or of tragedy, or indeed whether it fell outside formal expectations of genre. He would have needed to devise climactic scenes, and to think about how to bring the action to a satisfyingly dramatic conclusion.

The ground plans for some of his plays are more schematically worked out than others. *Much Ado About Nothing*, for instance (first printed I believe from his original manuscript) has an improvisatory air about it, as if at times we can catch him in the act of working out his plot as

10 'When we are born, we cry that we are come to this great stage of fools' (*King Lear*, 4.5.178–9). David Bradley as Gloucester and Robert Stephens as Lear in Adrian Noble's 1993 production.

he went along – the most obvious example is the presence in two stage directions of Hero's mother, Innogen, who does and says nothing. It is as if he had thought he might need her for the plot but eventually could think of nothing for her to say, or perhaps that he realized that he simply didn't have enough boy actors to include her. Some plays include substantial episodes inessential to the plot but offering entertaining interludes, such as Lance's scenes with his dog, Crab, in *The Two Gentlemen of Verona*, or reflection upon what has been happening, such as the scene of the gardeners discussing the state of the commonwealth in *Richard II* (3.4), or the dialogue between the mad Lear and the blind Gloucester (in *King Lear*, 4.5). Such scenes have been termed 'mirror scenes', and can illuminate the significances that Shakespeare derived from his stories. Other plays, however, such as *The Comedy of Errors*, *Romeo and Juliet*, and *The Tempest*, are elaborately and neatly plotted as if, like an architect designing a great cathedral, Shakespeare had created his overall design before going back to fill in the details. And there is no way in which the intricacies of the virtuosically designed final scene of *Cymbeline*, with its multiple denouements, can have been improvised on the spur of the moment. Its composition required the same kind of intellectual effort as a contrapuntal masterpiece by Bach.

In writing a comedy, Shakespeare would have wanted to devise scenes particularly productive of laughter – the overhearing scenes and the aborted pageant in *Love's Labour's Lost*, Malvolio appearing in cross-gartered yellow stockings in *Twelfth Night*, the gulling of Paroles in *All's Well That Ends Well*. And the conventions of comedy encouraged the inclusion of dances, of music and song. Here he would have required the collaboration of composers, instrumentalists, and singing actors. We know that some of his actors were musicians: Augustine Phillips, for instance, in his will of 1605 bequeathed 'a cittern, a bandora, and a lute' to one of his apprentices, and a bass viol (along with clothing and his sword and dagger) to a former apprentice.

For a tragedy Shakespeare would have wanted especially to give his actors the chance to portray passion, as Hamlet does, for example when he upbraids his mother, or Lear on the heath, or Othello in his jealous rage with Desdemona, or Coriolanus in his diatribes against the common people. But Shakespeare was not bound by convention, and his range and technique developed as he gained experience. He broadened generic expectations. Whereas for example his earlier comedies lack villains, he introduced comic antagonists – Shylock in *The Merchant of Venice*, Don John in *Much Ado About Nothing*, Duke Frederick and the unreformed Oliver in *As You Like It*, Malvolio in *Twelfth Night* – into his later romantic comedies. And later in his career he deepens the emotional range of comedy by portraying serious moral dilemmas in *Measure for Measure* and *All's Well That Ends Well*.

In doing all this he would keep at the forefront of his mind various practical considerations. He would need to remember how many actors he had available to him, and he would have to tailor the plot accordingly. Most of his plays can be performed by a company of fourteen actors if some of them take more than one role each. This required virtuosity among his actors, and seems sometimes to have placed strains upon his ingenuity. In *Romeo and Juliet*, for example, Lady Montague, Romeo's mother, might have been expected to be present in the final scene to share her husband's grief at their son's death, and to join, as Juliet's parents do, in the reconciliation of the two families, but when the Prince calls on her husband to join in the general mourning, he unexpectedly announces

> Alas, my liege, my wife is dead tonight.
> Grief of my son's exile hath stopped her breath.
>
> (5.3.209–10)

Somewhat similarly, in the final scene of *Twelfth Night*, although we learn that Sir Toby has married Maria, she is not brought on to share in the scene of Malvolio's discomfiture which she has helped to engineer. It seems likely that both of these characters suffer from what we may call Chronic Short-age of Boy Actors Syndrome.

He would limit the number of female roles according to the number of boys in the company at any given time – most of his plays call for no more than four, *Hamlet* and *Julius Caesar* need only two – and he needed to be sure that the roles he wrote for them were within their capacities. At some stages of his career he demonstrates exceptional confidence in boy actors' abilities: both *As You Like It* and *Twelfth Night*, for instance, written close together, call for a well-matched pair of accomplished boys to play respectively the substantial roles of Rosalind and Celia and of Viola and Olivia. And the role of Cleopatra is so complex that some people – especially mature female actors of our own time – have questioned whether it would have been played by a boy (however precisely we define the term).

He would want to write starring roles for the leading actors, and in doing so both to cater for their strengths and to remember their limitations. It is noticeable, for example, that none of the parts that Richard Burbage, star of the company throughout Shakespeare's career, is known to have played requires him to display any talent in singing – indeed the role of Benedick makes a joke out of his vocal limitations (5.5.229), though the demands made of for example Romeo and Hamlet show that Shakespeare had confidence in the actor's swordsmanship. And though he displays great confidence in the staying power of his leading players he learned to be considerate to them too – whereas Richard III has little respite during the course of his play, the heroes of later plays such as Hamlet, Macbeth, and Lear all have time off in their plays' later stages for a rest – or even a short nap – to help them to summon up strength to play their closing scenes.

To say that Shakespeare would have to do all this is not, of course, to suggest that the writing of a play for the theatre of his time was any more difficult for him than for any of his fellow playwrights. Nor should it imply that he was simply a journeyman writing plays to order. He was driven by internal compulsions, by changing and developing creative urges as well as by practical considerations. But it does seem desirable in thinking about his mental capacities and the demands that his profession made upon him to emphasize the fact that the composition of plays for the theatres of his time made great demands on a writer's intellectual resources, and that the peculiar circumstances of the conditions under which Shakespeare was working were especially demanding.

How Did Shakespeare Compose?

Once the play was plotted, a ground plan constructed, the dialogue had to be written. How fluent was Shakespeare? No working papers for any of the canonical plays survive. His colleagues Heminges and Condell, in their preface to the First Folio, wrote that 'His mind and hand went together: and what he thought, he uttered with that easiness that we have scarce received from him a blot in his papers.' I don't put much faith in this statement. Most of the plays in the Folio were printed not from Shakespeare's manuscripts – his 'papers' – but from annotated copies of already printed quartos or from scribal transcripts. Still, what his colleagues say is consonant with the evidence provided by his only surviving literary manuscript, the 180 or so lines that he is believed to have added to the multi-authored play of *Sir Thomas More* after it had been subjected, at an uncertain date, to censorship by the Master of the Revels, Edmund Tilney.

This is the only literary manuscript – indeed the only example of Shakespeare's handwriting except for a few signatures on legal documents – to have survived. In it there is scarcely any punctuation, as if his ideas were flowing with such facility that he had no time to bother about details. Words are often abbreviated, to save time. The spelling is fluid, as was characteristic of the period – our word 'sheriff' is spelt in five different ways within as many lines. Three consecutive lines are 'blotted' with substitutions made between the deleted lines. This is a man in a hurry, writing probably to commission to patch up a manuscript play after the Master of the Revels had demanded extensive change for political reasons.

The most revealing example of a passage of dialogue from a printed play that is preserved in both unrevised and revised forms is to be found in a long speech delivered by Biron in *Love's Labour's Lost*. The manuscript that went to the printer clearly had not been thoroughly prepared for publication. Shakespeare started by writing:

> From women's eyes this doctrine I derive.
> They are the grounds, the books, the academes,
> From whence doth spring the true Promethean fire.
> Why, universal plodding poisons up
> The nimble spirits in our arteries,
> As motion and long-during action tires
> The sinewy vigour of the traveller.

> Now, for not looking on a woman's face
> You have in that forsworn the use of eyes,
> And study too, the causer of your vow.
> For where is any author in the world
> Teaches such beauty as a woman's eye?
> Learning is but an adjunct to ourself,
> And where we are our learning likewise is.
> Then when ourselves we see in ladies' eyes,
> With ourselves,
> Do we not likewise see our learning there?

The speech opens well but loses impetus. It shows Shakespeare drawing readily on contemporary physiological theory in 'the nimble spirits in the arteries', on his classical knowledge in 'Promethean fire', and on his experience as a seasoned horseman with well-developed thigh muscles and accustomed to making long journeys in the reference to 'long-during action' that 'tires the sinewy vigour of the traveller'. There is an awkward break after the tenth line: 'and study too, the causer of your vow' is unrelated to what precedes and follows it; and the repetition in 'a woman's eye' and 'ladies' eyes' is clumsy. The passage peters out at the end as if Shakespeare knew that he had got himself into a tangle. So he starts afresh, seeing the opportunity for many improvements on the way, and producing a wonderfully exhilarating paean in praise of love which, he writes,

> ... first learnèd in a lady's eyes,
> Lives not alone immurèd in the brain,
> But with the motion of all elements
> Courses as swift as thought in every power,
> And gives to every power a double power

Above their functions and their offices.
It adds a precious seeing to the eye—
A lover's eyes will gaze an eagle blind.
A lover's ear will hear the lowest sound
When the suspicious head of theft is stopped.
Love's feeling is more soft and sensible
Than are the tender horns of cockled snails.
Love's tongue proves dainty Bacchus gross in taste.
For valour, is not love a Hercules,
Still climbing trees in the Hesperides?
Subtle as Sphinx, as sweet and musical
As bright Apollo's lute strung with his hair;
And when love speaks, the voice of all the gods
Make heaven drowsy with the harmony.   (4.1.294–312)

The evident revision here disproves the idea, reported by Ben Jonson, that Shakespeare 'never blotted line'. Here he has 'blotted' at least seventeen lines. But it supports the view that his verse could flow 'with great facility' once he got into full swing. Still, there are many passages of complex, even crabbed verse in his plays – especially later ones such as *Troilus and Cressida* and *Cymbeline* – which show him struggling with difficult ideas and not always appearing to be totally on top of his material.

Putting the Text into Production

There had to come a point at which Shakespeare turned over his final manuscript – his 'fair copy' – to a scribe who would have the responsibility of making one or more full copies of it for use in the theatre – by a prompter, for instance – and by writing out each actor's part individually so that the play could be put into rehearsal. 'Have you the lion's part written?' says Snug in *A Midsummer Night's Dream*. 'Pray you, if it be, give it me, for I am slow of study' (1.2.62–63). Since he has nothing to do but roar he's told he doesn't need a script – though he would need to learn his cues, in order to roar in the appropriate places.

Normally, plays were acted before they were printed. Each actor would have only his own part, all his speeches written out on a scroll with only a few words of the cue line to indicate when he had to come in. Very few such scrolls survive, and none for any of Shakespeare's plays. The most substantial is for a role in Robert Greene's *Orlando Furioso* of 1592 written for Edward Alleyn, the star of the Lord Admiral's Men, and even that is incomplete. It is made up of sheets of paper pasted together which would have made a document about seventeen feet long. It must have been unwieldy to manipulate; and the cue lines are very short. There are some stage directions. One can imagine the actor getting hopelessly and hilariously tangled up with it in rehearsal.

This method of putting on plays means that Shakespeare, as his company's resident playwright, is likely to have been deeply involved in the process of rehearsal and production, at least until the plays had become established among the company's repertory. An actor himself, he played roles in both his own and other people's plays. We don't know which roles he undertook, nor is there reason to suppose that he had great acclaim as an actor. But he would have been available during the rehearsal process to discuss possible changes to his scripts such as those I have mentioned in *A Midsummer*

Night's Dream, and we have reason to believe that he made, or at least acquiesced in, even more substantial revisions to several of his plays, including *Hamlet*, *Troilus and Cressida*, *Othello*, and *King Lear*, displayed in the substantial differences between their quarto and Folio texts. (There is also reason to believe that some of the plays printed in the Folio, especially *Measure for Measure* and *Macbeth*, were adapted by other hands, probably after Shakespeare died.) Shakespeare's revisions would have been made in consultation with the actors, who may well have contributed to them.

The scripts of his plays, then, were fluid; those that survive are as it were only snapshots taken at various periods of their evolution from first manuscripts through early production scripts through adaptation necessitated by varying conditions of performance and complicated by changes of their author's mind.

The processes by which Shakespeare composed his plays, and the extent, variety, and quality of his output, identify him as an immensely hard-working, practically minded man who could adapt himself to the working conditions of his time, seeing himself as one of a team, and willing to listen to voices other than his own. At the same time, the range and originality of his work show that he could challenge orthodoxy and transcend convention to produce dramas that stretch the limits of the medium in which he was working.

3 *What Do the Sonnets Tell Us about Their Author?*

S HAKESPEARE was primarily a public writer, an entertainer, a teller of tales about people other than himself, two of them – *Venus and Adonis* and *The Rape of Lucrece* – in narrative verse, but mostly dramas which cast only an oblique light on the mind and emotions of their writer. But he also wrote 154 individual, non-dramatic sonnets, almost all cast in the first person singular, as if they were personal utterances. They are at once some of the most famous, the most personally revealing, and the most badly misunderstood poems ever written.

Like many readers, I got to know some of the sonnets as an adolescent, attracted by their quintessentially romantic reputation – a bit like Abraham Slender in *The Merry Wives of Windsor* who, inarticulate at the prospect of wooing Anne Page, wishes he had his 'book of songs and sonnets here' (1.1.181–182). Much later I edited them for the Oxford Complete Works, published in 1986, and over the years I've written about them quite a lot: in for example the book I co-authored with Paul Edmondson for the Oxford Shakespeare Topics series published in 2004; in a number of essays published in *Shakespeare Survey* and elsewhere; and in another co-authored book, *All the Sonnets of Shakespeare*, published by Cambridge University Press in September 2020, which for the first time rearranges the sonnets of 1609 into a conjectural chronological order and intersperses them with passages in sonnet form from the plays. But I continue to find them fascinating and often enigmatic in themselves, in relation both to one another and to Shakespeare's life. Here, I want to address the much disputed question of how personal they are, what they tell us about their author.

First, a bit of background. As a literary form the sonnet was especially popular during the early years of Shakespeare's career – more indeed than at any other period in English literary history. Seventeen sequences of sonnets were published between 1591 and 1597, when the vogue came to a sudden end. Typically they are presented as coherent sequences, collections of poems addressed to or concerning one particular, sometimes identifiable woman who is unresponsive to her male lover's wooing. Varying in length from around 40 to 108 sonnets, none of them is anything like as long as the Shakespeare collection of 154 sonnets published in 1609 (which also includes the narrative poem 'A Lover's Complaint').

Shakespeare began writing sonnets during this period, both as stand-alone poems and as part of the poetic fabric of his plays. Current scholarly studies, many of them conducted by Macdonald P. Jackson, based on stylistic evidence suggest that Shakespeare wrote many of his independently written sonnets during the early to mid 1590s. In our co-edited volume *All the Sonnets of Shakespeare* Paul Edmondson and I draw attention to the fact that Shakespeare's most extensive deployment of sonnet form both in independent poems and in plays occurred simultaneously with the vogue for publishing sonnet sequences written by other poets. We do this by interspersing sonnets from the 1609 collection in their assumed chronological order of composition with the passages in sonnet form from plays generally believed to have been written between 1589 and 1596, including *Love's Labour's Lost*, *Romeo and Juliet*, and *A Midsummer Night's Dream*, while the vogue for publishing sonnet sequences was at its height. But there is one crucial difference. While the other writers may have been addressing a particular love object, often under a fictionalized name such as Celia, Delia, Phyllis, Diana, Fidessa, and so on, Shakespeare was writing privately, with apparently no intention of publication; and not a single one of his 154 sonnets names an addressee. The only sonnets by Shakespeare given to the public during this period are those that form part of his plays – sonnets such as those composed by the lords in *Love's Labour's Lost* as part of their wooing campaign, those that form the choruses to the first and second acts of *Romeo and Juliet*, and, most famously, that into which Shakespeare cast the first encounter of the lovers in that play (1.5.92–105).

But this does not mean that he was not writing independent sonnets during these years. Although his collection of sonnets did not appear till 1609, the very title of the book – *Shakespeare's Sonnets, never before imprinted* – clearly derives not from the author but from the publisher, and it draws attention to the fact that these poems are not new: they are – so the publisher hopes – long-awaited poems from a writer well enough known to be identifiable from his surname alone.

Shakespeare could certainly have found a publisher for sonnets long before 1609, as is clear from the fact that two sonnets by him did actually appear under his name but without his permission in a pirated publication, *The Passionate Pilgrim*, of 1598 or 1599. Slightly different versions of these two poems were to appear as Nos 138 and 144 in the collection published in 1609. It used to be supposed that the earlier printed versions were corrupt, but more recent thought suggests that they are printed in the form in which Shakespeare first wrote them, and that the 1609 versions represent his revisions.

The fact that these two sonnets appeared without their author's permission makes it reasonable to suggest that Shakespeare regarded his sonnets as private poems, written out of an impulse for self-expression rather than for publication. This impression is consonant with the first printed reference to any sonnets by Shakespeare, which appeared in 1598 in a book by the literary chronicler Francis Meres. In *Palladis Tamia* (*Wit's Treasury*) Meres wrote: 'The witty soul of Ovid lives in mellifluous and honey-tongued Shakespeare, witness his *Venus and Adonis*, his *Lucrece*, his sugared sonnets among his private friends, &c.' Curiously the phrase 'sugared sonnets' had been used in a cryptic poem published four years previously by Richard Barnfield, a friend of Meres and author of a number of charmingly light-hearted love poems addressed to a man, which forms part of Barnfield's sequence *Greene's Funerals* (1594). There, oddly referring it would seem to Marlowe as 'Malta's poet' – i.e. the author of *The Jew of Malta* – Barnfield writes that his own muse 'seldom sings' 'sugared sonnets'. The association of this phrase with the two best-known homoerotic poets of the period (other than Shakespeare) is intriguing; might 'sugared sonnets' have implied poems that were homoerotic in tone? (We should bear in mind that the sonnets that Meres knew about are not necessarily among those that have survived.)

Meres was certainly correct in identifying Ovid as a major influence on Shakespeare's narrative poems: *Venus and Adonis* bears a quotation from Ovid's *Amores* on its title page, and the poem derives its story from the *Metamorphoses*, just as *Lucrece* is based mainly on Ovid's historical poem *Fasti*. And although Shakespeare's sonnets are among his least derivative writings, they contain echoes of Ovid in, especially, the opening lines of Sonnet 60:

> Like as the waves make towards the pebbled shore,
> So do our minutes hasten to their end,
> Each changing place with that which goes before,
> In sequent toil all forwards do contend.

This is clearly influenced by Golding's translation of Ovid's *Metamorphoses* Book 15, especially lines 178–206:

> In all the world there is not that that standeth at a stay.
> Things ebb and flow, and every shape is made to pass
> away.
> The time itself continually is fleeting like a brook,
> For neither brook nor lightsome time can tarry still. But
> look
> As every wave drives other forth, and that that comes
> behind
> Both thrusteth and is thrust itself, even so the times by
> kind
> Do fly and follow both at once and evermore renew,
> For that that was before is left, and straight there doth
> ensue
> Another that was never erst …

The sonnet form, made popular in Italy by Dante and Petrarch, is especially associated with love poetry. Ovid wrote before the form was invented, but he was celebrated as the supreme poet of love, especially in his series *Amores*, which had been beautifully and wittily translated by Marlowe as *Elegies* at some time during the 1580s – they circulated widely in manuscript but versions ostensibly printed abroad and circulated surreptitiously in England were condemned to be burned by the Bishops' Ban of 1599 because they were regarded as obscene.

At the time Meres was writing, in 1598, no non-dramatic sonnet by Shakespeare had appeared in print. Clearly Meres had inside knowledge; he may have known Shakespeare personally. At any rate he had somehow got to know that Shakespeare was writing 'sugared' sonnets. What exactly he meant by 'private friends' is unclear. Did he mean that Shakespeare had written sonnets to commission by unidentified patrons? It is often suggested (absurdly in my view) that the first seventeen as printed in 1598, all of which encourage a young man to marry, might have been written to order from the young man's mother. Or had Meres perhaps learnt that Shakespeare had addressed poems privately to a patron – such as the young Earl of Southampton – or to one or more other, less socially prominent persons?

The two sonnets published in *The Passionate Pilgrim* and later in the 1609 collection (as Sonnets 138 and 144) are highly intimate poems concerning their author's – or at least their imaginary speaker's – sex life which, if we read them autobiographically, their author might well have preferred to be read only by his 'private friends' – or even to keep to himself. Deeply serious, even introverted in tone, they read to me more like a man's private attempts to wrestle with his inner demons than to entertain or charm a paying public. Circulation of poems in manuscript was common at the time, but if, as I suspect, these are really poems that their author preferred to keep under wraps, the fact that they nevertheless got into print suggests either that he must have been astonishingly indiscreet in allowing them to be copied, or that one or more members of his inner circle must have betrayed his confidence.

It seems worth taking a close look at both these poems since they appear to show Shakespeare thinking deeply about intimately personal predicaments.

The 1598 version of Sonnet 138 reads (in modernized spelling):

> When my love swears that she is made of truth
> > I do believe her though I know she lies,
> That she might think me some untutored youth
> > Unskilful in the world's false forgeries.
> Thus vainly thinking that she thinks me young,
> > Although I know my years be past the best,
> I, smiling, credit her false-speaking tongue,
> > Outfacing faults in love with love's ill rest.
> But wherefore says my love that she is young,
> > And wherefore say not I that I am old?
> O, love's best habit's in a soothing tongue,
> > And age in love loves not to have years told.
> > > Therefore I'll lie with love, and love with me,
> > > Since that our faults in love thus smothered be.

This is an intimate, psychologically complex, tortuously expressed poem which I will paraphrase as clearly as I can.

The poet complains that when the woman he loves says she's totally trustworthy he pretends to believe her even though he knows 'she lies'. And he deceives himself into appearing to believe that she thinks he's younger and less experienced than he really is, knowing nothing of worldly deceits. He blandly pretends to himself as well as to her that he believes her 'false-speaking tongue', putting a brave face on lovers' deceits with a lover's troubled mind. But, he asks, why does she say she's younger than she really is, and why doesn't he admit that he's old? Lovers do best to appear to trust one another even when they don't really do so, and people in love don't like to admit that they are as old as they really are. So he will lie – meaning both 'speak untruthfully' and 'lie down' – with love (in the abstract, and also with his lover), and she with him, because that is a way of concealing their faults as lovers.

Whatever else this is, it is not a 'sugared' sonnet in any obvious sense, nor is it obviously written out of lyrical impulse. It appears to be a cryptically private rather than a public poem, and if it is autobiographical it is a poem that its author might well have preferred to keep to himself, especially if there was any likelihood that the woman might see it. At the time it appeared, in 1599 – when it may not have been new – Shakespeare, writing of himself as 'old', was aged thirty-five – scarcely 'old' in our terms, though possibly relatively so at his time in relation to a much younger woman. I suppose it could have been entirely fictional, but it doesn't sound in the least like, for example, a speech from a play.

The other sonnet in the 1599 collection is a variant of one printed in 1609 (Sonnet 144). Jaggard's version reads:

> Two loves I have, of comfort and despair,
>   That like two spirits do suggest me still.
> My better angel is a man right fair,
> My worser spirit a woman coloured ill.
>   To win me soon to hell my female evil
> Tempteth my better angel from my side,
>   And would corrupt my saint to be a devil,
> Wooing his purity with her fair pride.
>   And whether that my angel be turned fiend,
> Suspect I may, yet not directly tell;
>   For being both to me, both to each friend,
> I guess one angel in another's hell.
>   The truth I shall not know, but live in doubt
>   Till my bad angel fire my good one out.

Again, this is no conventionally lyrical utterance. Sexually explicit like its partner, it is based on the medieval concept of a conflict for a man's soul between good and bad angels, as in a morality play, and it proclaims the author to have both a male and a female lover. Let me attempt a paraphrase:

I have two lovers, one comforting, the other that makes me despair, who continually, like two spirits, tempt me. The better is a handsome man, the worse a woman 'coloured ill' (whatever exactly that may mean). My female evil spirit tempts my better angel away from me in order to condemn me to hell, and seeks to corrupt my saintly friend to be a devil, seducing his purity with her enticing sexuality. And though I may suspect but cannot know for certain that my (male) angel has become a devil, I can't be sure, because since both of them are friends with both me and one another, I guess that each is occupying the other's intimate spaces. (The word 'hell' could refer to the vagina.) I shall not know the truth, but must live in suspicion until my bad angel (the woman) expels my good one (the man, by infecting him with venereal disease).

If we read this poem autobiographically then we must unequivocally regard Shakespeare as both heterosexually adulterous and bisexual, in love at once with a handsome man and an ill-favoured but sexually enticing woman. Moreover his statement of this had been made public. He had, as it were, been outed. Around the time he was preparing to write *Hamlet*, soon after he was asserting his respectability and his prosperity by buying the largest house in the borough of Stratford-upon-Avon, William Jaggard published poems, apparently without his permission, in which he declares himself a bisexual and an emotionally troubled adulterer.

By 1599, then, the reading public knew first hand from Francis Meres and at second hand from *The Passionate Pilgrim* that Shakespeare had written an unknown number of sonnets, and were able to read versions of two of them, both erotic, without necessarily knowing that others existed.

But more were to come. The book *Shakespeare's Sonnets* published in 1609 is not expensively or elegantly produced: many of the poems run clumsily over the page with awkward breaks. Moreover it contains a deliberately cryptic dedication which appears over the initials of the publisher – Thomas Thorpe – not the author, as we should expect, and as is true of the narrative poems *Venus and Adonis* and *The Rape of Lucrece*, of 1593 and 1594. There are many other puzzles here. Why is the dedication laid out like a tombstone with a dot after each word? Who is Mr W. H., and why is he identified only by his initials? What does 'only begetter' mean? The inspirer? The procurer of the manuscript? Both? The

TO.THE.ONLIE.BEGETTER.OF.
THESE.INSVING.SONNETS.
Mr.W.H. ALL.HAPPINESSE.
AND.THAT.ETERNITIE.
PROMISED.

BY.

OVR.EVER-LIVING.POET.

WISHETH.

THE.WELL-WISHING.
ADVENTVRER.IN.
SETTING.
FORTH.

T. T.

11 Dedication to *Shakespeare's Sonnets*, 1609. The cryptic dedication, shaped like a tombstone, is oddly printed in capital letters with a dot after each word over the initials only of the publisher rather than the author, and mysteriously refers by initials only to an 'only begetter'– Mr W. H. – of the poems.

phrase 'that eternity promised by our ever-living poet' would support the idea that he is the person addressed in some, at least, of the poems, which do indeed claim to immortalize the beloved. Why does Thorpe call himself a 'well-wishing adventurer'? Does he mean simply the 'well-disposed publisher' who takes a risk in issuing a book that may not sell well, or is there more to it than that? The dedication was written at a time when adventuring mariners were setting forth on dangerous voyages in search of wealth, rather as Antonio in *The Merchant of Venice* sends forth ships to foreign lands. Is this a clue to a hidden meaning?

The phrase 'never before imprinted' (not true, obviously, of the two sonnets that had appeared in *The Passionate Pilgrim*) implies that the poems were known to have existed for some time – as it were, Here they are at last! And this is in line with what we know or can reasonably conjecture about the dates at which they were written.

Stylistic studies suggest that the bulk of the poems published in the Shakespeare volume had been written while the vogue for sonnet sequences was at its height, early in his career, from about 1593 onwards, when Shakespeare was making most use of the form in his plays. The latest printed (Sonnets 127 to 154) are believed to be among the earliest composed, followed chronologically by Sonnets 1 to 103. The latest composed – Sonnets 104 to 126 – date from between 1600 and 1604 – all well before they were first published. Shakespeare may have gone on tinkering with individual poems in the years after he wrote them, especially while he was transcribing them into the version in which they eventually appeared in print.

This means that the 1609 order of printing is not the order in which the poems were written. But it is not entirely haphazard. The poems do not form an orderly 'sequence', although this term is often misleadingly applied to them by analogy with the sonnet sequences of the 1590s. It reflects and creates serious misunderstanding. A more accurate term is 'collection'. Nevertheless some of the poems run on in sense from one to the next, and others fall into pairs or mini-sequences related by subject matter: for instance, as I have said, the first seventeen all exhort a young man, or 'boy', to marry. Poems in which the writer mentions other, unidentified rival poets, include Sonnets 78 to 80, 82 to 86, and are grouped together.

False assumptions, which started towards the end of the eighteenth century, and which result from comparisons with sonnet sequences of the 1590s, are responsible for the frequently repeated statement that all the poems in the first group concern a male person, and that all those from No. 126 onwards are about a 'dark lady' – the term itself does not occur – a 'woman coloured ill', as she is called in No. 144. In fact only twenty of the poems, all in the first group, can confidently be said, on the evidence of forms of address and masculine pronouns, to be addressed to, or to concern, a male, while seven, all in the second group, are clearly about a 'dark' female ('dark' in facial features and perhaps in other respects). In the sonnets clearly addressed to a male he is variously addressed or mentioned as 'sweet', and in some of them the addressee's youth is emphasized: 'tender churl' (Sonnet 1), 'sweet boy' (Sonnet 108), and 'my lovely boy' (Sonnet 126). This enhances the possibility that the poems concern more than one male person.

There is a break towards the end of the collection. Sonnet 126 is in rhymed couplets and has only twelve lines, instead of the usual fourteen, followed cryptically by two pairs of empty brackets. All the poems concerned with a woman follow it, mixed up with others that are not. Some-one had clearly imposed a degree of order upon a collection of poems written at diverse dates.

So there are two very basic questions. One is, who arranged these poems, written at a variety of dates, some individually, others in pairs or clusters, into the order in which they appeared in print? It must have been someone who knew all the poems intimately and had thought hard about their relationship to one another. Shakespeare himself seems the obvious candidate. The other question is, if some or all of the poems are concerned with real people, who are these people?

We should like to have answers to the questions that the volume raises if only because they would help us to know what their author was really like. If, for example, he cold-bloodedly handed over for publication – for ready money – love poems addressed to and concerned with persons still living who would have known he was putting their intimate relationships into the public domain (even if they could not be easily identified), that would suggest a serious lack of concern for their feelings. If the printed text of the sonnets derives, directly or by way of a scribal transcript, from Shakespeare's own manuscript then it would appear that he had manuscripts of all 154 of them, that he had transcribed them into a single notebook, as if for his personal use – a bit like a boy collecting stamps, or more seriously like someone who writes poems with no expectation of publication but enjoys writing them out in their best handwriting, for private perusal or perhaps to be shown only to selected 'private friends'. But we don't know how the poems got into print.

The best we can do is examine the evidence and form our own conclusions from what it tells us. My conclusion, for what it is worth, is that Thorpe got hold by underhand means of a manuscript into which all the poems had been transcribed, probably by their author, certainly in an order that Shakespeare approved and which Thorpe followed; that the publisher's dedication is deliberately cryptic and may be addressed to some individual not in the public eye; and that Shakespeare disapproved of the publication but kept quiet about it, possibly so as not to draw attention to it.

On the surface, because of the phrasing of the title page and the dedication by the publisher rather than by the author, it seems that such a manuscript came into Thorpe's hands without Shakespeare's approval. But some scholars argue that Shakespeare himself handed over the poems to Thorpe for publication – presumably in return for money – and that the reason that Thorpe rather than Shakespeare wrote the dedication and supervised publication is because the author was unavailable – Katherine Duncan-Jones suggests that he had left London to escape the plague (but presumably that Thorpe bravely (or foolhardily) stayed put) – and that he gave Thorpe a free hand as to the details of their appearance. It has even been suggested that Shakespeare held publication back till 1609 for reasons of delicacy until his mother had died – in September 1608 – but one might suppose that he had more to fear from his wife's reactions, and she outlived him and could well have known of the book. (Even if she couldn't read it herself, some kind friend might well have told her about it.)

༄༅

In 1609, aged forty-five, Shakespeare was coming towards the end of his playwriting career. What Thorpe published in that year is an extraordinarily diverse collection of poems – and their very diversity distinguishes them from the sonnet sequences of the 1590s, which are far more uniform in tone and content. Shakespeare's sonnets, written over a period of some twenty or more years, vary in content and style from the impersonal through the lyrical, the meditative, the celebratory, the apparently autobiographical to the opaquely intimate and the confessional, and, as we have seen, they include at the end two which are simply revised and unrevised versions of a translated paraphrase of a poem from a collection of fifth- or sixth-century poems known as the Greek Anthology which had been translated into Latin in the sixteenth century. We don't know how Shakespeare came upon the original, but it is conceivable that these are early essays in translation dating back to his schooldays.

Most, though not all, of the 1609 sonnets are written in the first person singular, or at least from the author's point of view. Some are as it were 'public' poems, which could have been written as poetical exercises or professionally, as potential contributions to poetic anthologies. But other sonnets are far more private utterances, containing cryptic references to public or even personal events which would have been unintelligible to readers unacquainted with intimate details of the poet's life. This surely suggests that these poems were written as a form of self-expression, or self-exploration, rather than for professional reasons.

The first group of poems in the volume, Sonnets 1 to 17, are closely related in that all of them are addressed to a beautiful, unnamed young man whom the poet urges to marry. It has been suggested that they were written to commission from a mother anxious that her son seemed not to be facing up to his duty of perpetuating the family line, but they imply a degree of intimacy between the poet and the person addressed that goes far beyond the formal. The poet addresses the young man as 'love' (Sonnet 13), and goes so far as to beg him, in veiled but surely unmistakable terms, to stop masturbating and to start propagating:

> Thou that art now the world's fresh ornament
>   And only herald to the gaudy spring
> Within thine own bud buriest thy content
>   And, tender churl, mak'st waste in niggarding

– that is, paradoxically, behave wastefully by keeping your seed to yourself (Sonnet 1). And again – from Sonnet 4:

> having traffic with thyself alone
> Thou of thyself thy sweet self dost deceive.

Is this how a poet might address a man he was simply being paid to advise? The situation portrayed may seem paradoxical: a mature man who loves a beautiful young man nevertheless urges him to marry a woman, as if against the poet's personal desires. Perhaps it could be explained if the addressee were someone – like, dare I say, Shakespeare's patron the Earl of Southampton, who was rumoured to have had a sexual relationship with one of his officers while serving on the Irish campaign of 1597, and whose social position required him to marry whatever his personal inclinations. But whatever the biographical situation may have been, it precipitated poems which give abiding lyrical expression to the emotions of a lover and of any human being contemplating the effects of time on 'everything that grows' (Sonnet 15).

Here's Sonnet 12:

When I do count the clock that tells the time,
    And see the brave day sunk in hideous night;
When I behold the violet past prime,
    And sable curls all silvered o'er with white;
When lofty trees I see barren of leaves
    Which erst from heat did canopy the herd,
And summer's green all girded up in sheaves
    Borne on the bier with white and bristly beard,
Then of thy beauty do I question make,
    That thou among the wastes of time must go,
Since sweets and beauties do themselves forsake
    And die as fast as they see others grow;
      And nothing 'gainst time's scythe can make defence
      Save breed, to brave him when he takes thee hence.

Whatever occasioned it, that's a beautiful lyric on the passage of time, particularized in the sestet by being addressed to an unnamed person.

Many of the poems in the later part of the collection, too, show their author meditating on traditional themes of lyric poetry – the destructive effects of time on youth and beauty, the possibility that love and art may transcend time, the hope that the poet's verse may confer immortality upon the addressee. In this, though they may have had a topical purpose, they transcend it.

But some of the poems stand far outside the traditional boundaries of lyric verse in the intensity of their exploration of what appear to be deeply personal, even private issues. So for example Sonnet 129 is a profoundly serious poem in which the poet meditates in anguished terms on the consequences of yielding to lust without love.

> Th'expense of spirit in a waste of shame
>   Is lust in action; and till action, lust
> Is perjured, murderous, bloody, full of blame,
>   Savage, extreme, rude, cruel, not to trust;
> Enjoyed no sooner but despisèd straight;
>   Past reason hunted; and no sooner had,
> Past reason hated, as a swallowed bait
>   On purpose laid to make the taker mad:
> Mad in pursuit, and in possession so;
>   Had, having, and in quest to have, extreme;
> A bliss in proof, and proved, a very woe;
>   Before, a joy proposed; behind, a dream.
>   All this the world well knows; yet none knows well
>   To shun the heaven that leads men to this hell.

This poem would seem completely out of place in a conventional sonnet sequence of the period. It might be thought to resemble a meditation on a topic such as the actions of the rapist Tarquin in *Lucrece*, or the state of mind of Angelo lusting after Isabella in *Measure for Measure*; equally, it might express Shakespeare's personal experience of remorse and shame springing from consciousness that lust has driven him to self-betrayal.

The most profoundly personal, even confessional of the poems are to be found among the last-printed group, from 127 to 152 – it's tempting to call them a group, as they include all that are clearly addressed to a woman, but that applies to only seven of them. The poet speaks of his mistress – if indeed there is only one mistress – in conflicting and conflicted terms. 'My mistress' eyes are nothing like the sun' (130), which parodies the conventions of Petrarchan verse using a phrase also found in Sonnet 127: '*My mistress's eyes* are raven black' – denies her the conventional attributes of a poetical love object but ends with a declaration of love which is all the more powerful for the volte-face that it expresses:

> And yet, by heaven, I think my love as rare
> As any she belied with false compare.

There is also a small group of poems, Sonnets 78 to 86, which include references to a so-called 'rival poet' (or conceivably more than one such poet) who was a rival in the author's love. Many attempts, all fruitless, have been made to identify him with known poets of the period (among those suggested have been Christopher Marlowe, George Chapman, Ben Jonson, and other, lesser poets). Indeed Sonnet 86 alludes to a confederacy of rival collaborators, 'compeers by night'. Presumably these poems would have been as puzzling to readers of Shakespeare's time as they are to us, a fact that supports the idea that the sonnets are private poems.

The most explicitly autobiographical sonnets seem to be those that pun on the poet's first name – William. They are the only poems in the collection that give a personal name to any of the protagonists. 'My name is,' he declares unequivocally, 'Will' (136). Nowhere else does the poet identify himself so emphatically.

A number of these poems imply that the poet is involved in a triangular affair with another man and a woman. But other poems in this group are cryptic in allusions to a love triangle. Sonnet 133, for example, is expressive of a love–hate relationship that is totally at odds with conventional love poetry. Shakespeare, apparently addressing a woman and without identifying himself by name, speaks of the affair with anguish, and implies that both his male and his female lover have abandoned him in a manner that deprives him of his sense of identity:

> Me from myself thy cruel eye hath taken,
>   And my next self thou harder hast engrossed.
> Of him, myself, and thee I am forsaken –
>   A torment thrice threefold thus to be crossed.

Self-identification resumes with No. 135, beginning 'Whoever hath her wish, thou hast thy Will', which uses the word 'will' thirteen times, and does so, sometimes with grotesquely lewd punning, in at least five distinct senses: the poet's own name, desire, object of desire, vagina, and penis.

The poem that follows, No. 136, uses the word 'will' five times and ends 'my name is Will'. The next two, though they do not pun on 'will', continue the theme. In No. 137 the poet castigates himself for thinking 'that' – the woman's vagina – to be 'a several plot' – an exclusively owned territory – although his heart knows it to be 'the wide world's common place' – she is promiscuous; and in No. 138, admitting that he suppresses truth by 'believing' his mistress's lies, he acknowledges his folly with bitter puns: 'Therefore I lie with her, and she with me, / And in our lies by lies we flattered be.'

The harsh, explicit, and totally unsentimental sexual frankness of these poems, exceeding anything to be found in the sonnet sequences of the 1590s, and indeed of most of Elizabethan literature other than the avowedly pornographic, reaches a climax in No. 151, which portrays the poet's soul as giving him permission to permit his erect penis repeatedly to penetrate his woman friend:

> My soul doth tell my body that he may
> Triumph in love; flesh stays no farther reason,
> But rising at thy name doth point out thee
> As his triumphant prize. Proud of this pride,
> He is contented thy poor drudge to be,
> To stand in thy affairs, fall by thy side.
> No want of conscience hold it that I call
> Her 'love' for whose dear love I rise and fall.

I think it can safely be said that no sonnet of the period – or indeed of most other periods – approaches this in its explicit – in this case, heterosexual – sexuality. It is powerfully eloquent in for example the enjambment of the first two and the third and fourth lines; in the rhythmic regularity of the first and the inverted opening foot of the second line; in the alliteration of 'flesh' and 'farther' and of 'prize … Proud … pride'; and in the rhythmic inversion of 'fall by thy side' which creates an impression of detumescence. Masterly in technique, this poem gives us exceptional access to Shakespeare's sexual imagination.

12 Sonnet 151. Simon Brett's wood engraving matches
Shakespeare's poem in its sexual explicitness. The half-naked
lovers look away from one another as if in shame, linked by a cord
around their necks apparently attached to lockets bearing portraits
of two men, and by the woman's hand masturbating Shakespeare.

In the midst of all this tormented sexual self-
examination and overt sexuality, which would be obscene
were it not so earnest, comes, incongruously, Shakespeare's
only religious poem (except perhaps for the obscurely mys-
tic 'Phoenix and Turtle'), Sonnet 146, beginning 'Poor soul,
the centre of my sinful earth'. There seems to be no reason
why we should not accept this poem, which is as solid in its
affirmation of spiritual over worldly values as any of the mag-
nificent Holy Sonnets of John Donne (which circulated only
in manuscript during Donne's lifetime), as Shakespeare's

personal affirmation of religious belief. (Regrettably, in the 1609 edition the last three words of the first line were accidentally repeated as the first three of the second line.)

> Poor soul, the centre of my sinful earth,
>   […] these rebel powers that thee array;
> Why dost thou pine within and suffer dearth,
>   Painting thy outward walls so costly gay?
> Why so large cost, having so short a lease,
>   Dost thou upon thy fading mansion spend?
> Shall worms, inheritors of this excess,
>   Eat up thy charge? Is this thy body's end?
> Then, soul, live thou upon thy servant's loss,
>   And let that pine to aggravate thy store.
> Buy terms divine in selling hours of dross;
>   Within be fed, without be rich no more.
>   So shalt thou feed on death, that feeds on men,
>   And death once dead, there's no more dying then.

This poem, which speaks against the kind of personal display associated with theatre, may well express a creed to which Shakespeare adhered throughout his life. It shows that he could empathize with religious believers, and it should not be ignored in attempts to assess his religious faith.

To sum up, then, it seems to me that the Sonnets are a highly diverse collection of poems with varying degrees of relevance to Shakespeare's personal and public life. The last two in the collection as printed, both derived from the same Greek epigram, are literary exercises in the purest sense. Two of the poems (21 and 130) parody the sonnet convention. One sonnet – 146 – is a religious meditation, another – 129, beginning 'Th'expense of spirit in a waste of shame' – a philosophical study on a sexual theme. Some of the poems are not particularly personal and would be at home in any collection of love poetry of the period. Others may be more or less identifiably related to Shakespeare's personal experience but would nevertheless have been intelligible and enjoyable to contemporary readers who did not know him. One – the Hathaway poem, No. 145 – is identifiable as a personal love poem. The sonnets advocating marriage – 1 to 17 – seem to me to be poems written altruistically to a young man whom Shakespeare loves deeply but with no expectation of physical reciprocity. And finally there are sonnets that seem so intimately personal, not to say confessional, that I find it difficult not to see them as highly original poems that are autobiographical in origin and which Shakespeare wrote primarily for himself, to help him clarify his mind and emotions about personal dilemmas and rivalries in love.

These poems reveal a man who was at various times of his life caught up in emotional and sexual entanglements with more than one male – men, or boys, or (as Malvolio says of Viola) 'in standing water between boy and man' (*Twelfth Night*, 1.5.154), one of whom was also a poet – and with more than one woman; a man of conscience who experienced transcendent joy and happiness in love but who suffered as the result of other people's infidelities, who understood the pangs of physical separation and emotional estrangement from the beloved, and who was tormented with profound jealousy, guilt, and remorse about his own behaviour. 'That she that makes me sin awards me pain', he writes in Sonnet

141; 'Love is my sin', and his mistress's lips 'have [in Sonnet 142] sealed false bonds of love as oft as mine, / Robbed others' beds' revenues of their rents'.

Among all Shakespeare's writings the Sonnets, in all their diversity of moods and their profound introspection, bring us closest to a sense of what Shakespeare was really like. In this sense they form a kind of emotional autobiography. And they suggest that, even when he was asserting bourgeois respectability with his rising social status in Stratford and his artistic success in London, he was experiencing an inner life of at least intermittent emotional turmoil and sexual tension which found release in poetic composition. It should not surprise us if he wished to keep his sonnets to himself.

4   *What Made Shakespeare Laugh?*

For the last chapter I decided that I wanted to write about Shakespeare's sense of humour. I thought I would write about how – if at all – it is possible to know what made him smile and laugh. And I wanted to think about how this relates to our sense of his overall personality and of how that changed and developed over the years. But when I started actually to try to write the chapter, I began to think it would be a great deal easier to write a whole, rather long book about the subject than to try to encompass it within a single chapter. I also felt surprise that, so far as I know, no such book exists. Perhaps that is because it is easier to talk and write about tragedy, which we all know is a very serious matter, than about comedy, which it's too easy to think of as a trivial matter.

It is easiest to know what Shakespeare finds funny when he is writing as if in his own person, as in his poems rather than in his plays. There is obvious wit in *Venus and Adonis*, where he clearly delights in the irony of the goddess of love's failure to seduce the handsome but adolescent Adonis, even though he also allows the young man the self-defence of acknowledged emotional immaturity: 'Before I know myself seek not to know me' (line 525). And there

13 *We Three Loggerheads* (*c.* 1600–25). This portrait reputedly
showing Archie Armstrong and Muckle John, court fools to
King James I, shows them with the traditional coxcombs and a
bauble; either it or the viewer may be the third 'loggerhead'. The
image can be associated with the fool Feste's line 'Did you never
see the picture of "we three"?' in *Twelfth Night, or what you will.*

are comic touches such as the picture of Adonis yielding
momentarily to Venus's demand for a kiss:

> Upon this promise did he raise his chin,
>   Like a divedapper peering through a wave,
> Who being looked on, ducks as quickly in.
>   So offers he to give what she did crave,
> But when her lips were ready for his pay,
> He winks and turns his lips another way.   (lines 85–90)

It's quite like a moment from a film, isn't it? The image of a handsome young man peering upwards like a dabchick raising its head above the surface of what must surely in Shakespeare's mind have been the River Avon, and instantly plopping back again, has an irresistibly comic quality, and it's fair enough to identify the comic viewpoint with that of the author.

There are elements of satire and parody too in some of the sonnets. '*My* mistress' eyes are nothing like the sun' says Shakespeare in Sonnet 130, in a take-off of the conventional hyperbole of the traditional sonneteer. Clearly as he wrote these works he had a keen sense of irony, an awareness of the absurdity of the exaggerations of those who 'suffer love' (as Beatrice puts it in *Much Ado About Nothing*, 5.2.59).

When we come to the plays things become more complex. He liked to make people laugh. His earliest sole-authored play, I believe, was a comedy – *The Two Gentlemen of Verona* – and many more were to follow. As his career developed he became in an increasingly strong position to set his own agenda, not necessarily following theatrical fashion. It is notable, for example, that he continued to write romantic comedies for several years after the vogue for citizen comedies was inaugurated in 1598 with *Englishmen for My Money, or A Woman Will Have Her Will* by William Haughton, and by Ben Jonson's *Every Man in His Humour* (in the first performance of which Shakespeare himself acted). *The Merry Wives of Windsor*, which is difficult to date, may nod towards the new fashion, but it is set vaguely in the past rather than in Shakespeare's own time, and has a thoroughly romantic ending.

Shakespeare's deployment of comic form is full of variety; every play has its distinct identity. He was never a writer of farce, a genre in which a dramatist's principal aim is

14 Lance and his dog, Crab. A watercolour by Richard Westall (1765–1836), a prolific artist with a speciality in book illustration. The servingman, Lance, despairs over the impassivity of his spaniel Crab in *The Two Gentlemen of Verona*.

to raise laughter, often at the expense of characterization. *The Merry Wives of Windsor* is sometimes reduced to a farce in production, but only at the expense of drastic and insensitive cutting along with overly broad acting. *The Two Gentlemen of Verona* combines broad comedy – especially in the moments with Lance and his incontinent dog, Crab – with the comedy of situation that culminates unexpectedly in an episode of attempted rape. *The Comedy of Errors*, acted in 1594, is, as I have said, often treated as a farce in production but in fact it combines a highly sophisticated comedy of character and situation deriving from the Roman dramatist Plautus with the popular romance story of Apollonius of Tyre which Shakespeare was to dramatize again late in his career in *Pericles*. When I want to be provocative – as occasionally happens – I say that far from being a farce *The Comedy of Errors* is the first of Shakespeare's last plays.

It is true all the same that, although Shakespeare never abandons comedy, he wrote all his predominantly comic plays during the first half of his career, from whenever he started – sometime around 1590 – till about 1600. The lightest-hearted comedies, *The Two Gentlemen of Verona*, *The Taming of the Shrew*, *The Comedy of Errors*, *Love's Labour's Lost*, and *A Midsummer Night's Dream* come early, probably up to about 1595. Some of these comedies include serious elements verging on the tragic. In *The Comedy of Errors* Egeon is saved from execution only by the semi-miraculous fact that his twin sons take refuge in an abbey presided over by a lady who turns out, with hilarious improbability, to be his long-lost wife. And at the conclusion of *Love's Labour's Lost*, a messenger of death overshadows and delays the lovers' coming together. Overall, however, these are the happiest of the comedies.

As I said in talking about how Shakespeare wrote a play, the next five comedies – *The Merchant of Venice*, *Much Ado About Nothing*, *The Merry Wives of Windsor*, *Twelfth Night*, and *As You Like It* – unlike the earlier ones – all include among their casts a comic antagonist – respectively: Shylock, Don John, Falstaff, Malvolio, and Oliver (plus the melancholy Jaques) – who casts shadows of varying shades of darkness over the mirth. *The Merry Wives of Windsor* is the lightest of these plays overall, but has its serious side in the threat that Falstaff's attempts at committing adultery pose to Page's and Ford's marriages and in the moving reconciliation of Master and Mistress Ford. I remember the poignancy which Ian Richardson, who had been brilliantly amusing in his disguise as Master Brook, brought to his reconciliation with his wife (in Clifford Williams's 1962 production for the Royal Shakespeare Company). It was as poignant as the reconciliation of Count and Countess at the end of Mozart's opera *The Marriage of Figaro*.

In each of the other comedies the antagonist is expelled from the happy ending but with varying degrees of severity. In *The Merchant of Venice* Shylock is mocked by Graziano and other characters and forced to convert to Christianity – a fate that might even have been regarded by some of Shakespeare's contemporaries as a blessing. At the end of *Much Ado About Nothing* Don John is lightly dismissed with the vague threat from Benedick 'Think not of him till tomorrow. I'll devise thee brave punishments for him'. In *Twelfth Night* Orsino recommends that Malvolio, in spite of his vicious threat 'I'll be revenged on the whole pack of you', shall nevertheless be entreated 'to a peace'. And in *As You Like It* Oliver, who starts off as a cardboard villain, repents with implausible but dramaturgically convenient suddenness and ends up being subsumed into the circle of happy lovers.

It is during this period too that Shakespeare makes most use of the conventions and techniques of comedy in plays based on English history, drawing primarily on his imagination for their comic episodes, above all those portraying Sir John Falstaff, who is also of course the central character of *The Merry Wives of Windsor*.

The turning point comes with or around the time of *Hamlet* – the chronology is uncertain – the most comic of the tragedies, and the only one with a hero who in happier circumstances might have starred in a romantic comedy. Hamlet the man is in a direct line from Biron of *Love's Labour's Lost*, through Benedick of *Much Ado About Nothing*, to Jaques of *As You Like It*. He uses his mordant wit to pierce through the bland compromises of Claudius, to diffuse Polonius's sycophancy, and to satirize Osric's affectations. And the gravediggers' down-to-earth reality about the hard facts of death provokes a great burst of Hamlet's hectic imaginings.

As Shakespeare grows older his use of comic form becomes darker, more deeply fused with moral complexity and with the possibility, at least, of unhappy endings which, in the late romances, only near miracles or divine intervention can avert. Some of this may be attributable to external factors such as changes in dramatic fashion, collaboration with Thomas Middleton and John Fletcher, and the moral, even philosophical climate of the times. But it is natural to ask whether the darkening of the dramatist's palette reflects changes within Shakespeare himself. In this later part of his career all his plays in or approximating to comic form – *Measure for Measure*, *All's Well That Ends Well*, *Troilus and Cressida*, *Pericles*, *Cymbeline*, *The Winter's Tale*, and *The Tempest* – are deeply concerned with serious moral issues. In them the anti-comic forces, previously concentrated on a single figure, are more broadly diffused, and comic antagonists become more morally complex, more threatening, less easy to identify. He was getting older. Was he also becoming gloomier? Do the changes in his use of comic form reflect changes in his personality and in his response to life's events? Perhaps not: after all he went on writing comedies in the years immediately following the death of his son Hamnet in 1596, an event that might have been expected to darken his mood. Anyhow, even if he became less cheerful as the years passed, his creativity, so far from diminishing, grew in inventiveness, in emotional power, and in profundity. Maybe, as is true in a different medium with Beethoven, suffering brought him ever-growing depths of emotionally expressive power. It's as far a cry from the high spirits of Beethoven's first symphony to the profundity of his late quartets as it is from *The Comedy of Errors* to *The Winter's Tale*.

Whatever the truth about Shakespeare's later development and its inner causes, and however subtle and profound his use of comic resources became in his post-*Hamlet* period, it seems clear that in earlier years he felt that his natural bent was for comedy, and in the rest of this chapter I shall concentrate on this period.

We have to allow for the fact that dialogue apparently intended to amuse audiences may not directly reflect the author's own sense of humour; he may have hoped it might make other people laugh even if he himself found it unfunny. He may deliberately cause characters to make what we now might call 'groan jokes', where amusement arises from disbelief that anyone should be so stupid as to find them funny. Notoriously, some of the repartee in, especially, Shakespeare's early comedies is liable to strike modern audiences as forced and dated, and it may have had the same effect on Elizabethan playgoers. For instance, in *The Two Gentlemen of Verona* Lance, talking of the lovers – his master Proteus and Julia – says to his fellow servant Speed:

> Marry, thus: when it stands well with him, it
> stands well with her.
> SPEED What an ass art thou! I understand thee not.
> LANCE What a block art thou, that thou canst not! My
> staff understands me.
> SPEED What thou sayest?
> LANCE Ay, and what I do too: look thee, I'll but lean,
> and my staff understands me.
> SPEED It stands under thee, indeed.
> LANCE Why, stand-under and under-stand is all one.
>
> (2.5.20–29)

It seems likely that Shakespeare expected his audience to laugh at Lance for his simple-minded punning, and at Speed for his failure to see the joke, as well as to admire his own skill at portraying their naivety. Still, Shakespeare himself may have groaned as he wrote it.

Though he may have used devices to amuse his audiences which reflect his cold-blooded professionalism rather than revealing what would have aroused his own spontaneous laughter, it seems all the same to be worth trying to identify some of his principal comic techniques in the hope that these may cast at least an oblique light on his sense of humour.

He is, of course, notoriously especially fond of puns and wordplay. Dr Johnson famously wrote that 'A quibble [by which he meant a play on words] was to him the fatal Cleopatra for which he lost the world, and was content to lose it.' That sounds more like a rebuke than a compliment: clearly, punning jokes did not appeal to Johnson's neoclassical sympathy.

Wordplay takes many forms and can be variously complex. Shakespeare uses a simple form of it in revealing the pomposity and self-importance of a character such as Dogberry in *Much Ado About Nothing* as he responds to Conrad's assertion that he is an ass: 'Dost thou not suspect my place? Dost thou not suspect my years? O that he were here to write me down an ass!' (4.2.72–74).

It can be a fruitful source of bawdy comedy, and it may come from the lips of aristocrats and courtiers as well as of pimps and clowns. There is no filthier scene in Shakespeare than that in *Love's Labour's Lost*, Act 4, Scene 1, in which the clown Costard and the courtier Boyet comment jestingly on a conversation among the Princess's waiting women. Boyet, commenting on their proficiency in archery, says, 'A mark! O, mark but that mark! A mark, says my lady! Let the mark have a prick in't, to mete at, if it may be.' To which Maria replies:

'Wide a' the bow-hand! I' faith, your hand is out.' Costard comments, 'Indeed 'a must shoot nearer, or he'll ne'er hit the clout.' Boyet comes back at him with 'And if my hand be out, then belike your hand is in', and Costard says, 'Then will she get the upshoot by cleaving the pin' (which means, putting it simply, that she will cause him to ejaculate by masturbating him). It is no wonder that Maria then says, 'Come, come, you talk greasily, your lips grow foul.' It's worth remembering that these lines were written at the time when Shakespeare was also writing some of his Sonnets that are profoundly concerned with sexual dilemmas.

In post-Freudian times serious wordplay has come to be recognized as a means of evoking the workings of the subconscious mind and of suggesting the complexity of human experience. Shakespeare's use of the device grows in subtlety and depth; it is a far cry from Lance's 'My staff understands me' to Hamlet's 'Do you think I meant country matters?' (3.2.116), to the bitter wordplay of the Fool in *King Lear*, and to the dying Cleopatra's 'Husband, I come' (*Antony and Cleopatra*, 5.2.282) – if that is indeed intended as a pun.

From time to time Shakespeare employs anecdotes in which, often, the humour lies not just in the story itself but also in its aptness to the character of the person who tells it. These occur in the tragedies as well as in the comedies. In *Romeo and Juliet*, the Nurse's story of how her husband reacted when the infant Juliet fell over is funny because of the way it is told, and the light that this sheds on the Nurse's character, as much as for the inherent comedy of what happened: it shows us a Shakespeare who can use art – the speech is

written in blank verse (though it was first printed as prose) –
to depict artlessness:

> And then my husband – God be with his soul!
> He was a merry man – took up the child.
> 'Yea,' quoth he, 'Dost thou fall upon thy face?
> Thou wilt fall backward when thou hast more wit,
> Wilt thou not, Jule?' and, by my holy dame,
> The pretty wretch left crying and said 'ay.'
> To see now, how a jest shall come about!
> I warrant, an I should live a thousand years,
> I never should forget it. 'Wilt thou not, Jule?' quoth he.
> And, pretty fool, it stinted and said 'ay.'   (1.2.41–50)

In *The Merry Wives of Windsor*, Falstaff's rueful account of
how he was thrown into the River Thames along with the
dirty washing from a laundry basket is complicated by the
character's self-aware enjoyment of his discomfiture.

> 'Sblood, the rogues slighted me into the river with as little
> remorse as they would have drowned a blind bitch's pup-
> pies, fifteen i'th'litter! And you may know by my size that
> I have a kind of alacrity in sinking. If the bottom were as
> deep as hell, I should drown. I had been drowned, but that
> the shore was shelvy and shallow – a death that I abhor,
> for the water swells a man, and what a thing should I have
> been when I had been swelled? By the Lord, a mountain of
> mummy! (3.5.8–17)

The comedy of the speech derives partly from the fact that
Falstaff can see himself from the audience's point of view – he
is simultaneously the suffering victim of his plight and the
amused commentator on its ludicrous aspects.

15 The last scene of *The Merry Wives of Windsor*. A watercolour by John Massey Wright (1777–1866), a stage designer and prolific watercolourist specializing in book illustration. This drawing shows Falstaff being teased by children dressed as fairies and carrying torches.

Anecdotes may be emotionally complex, as in *Henry V* is Mistress Quickly's unwittingly bawdy and characteristically garrulous yet also intensely poignant account of the death of Falstaff. 'Falstaff, he is dead,' says Pistol, 'and we must earn [i.e. 'grieve'] therefore.' Bardolph says, 'Would I were with him, wheresome'er he is, either in heaven or in hell!', to which Mistress Quickly replies:

> Nay, sure, he's not in hell. He's in Arthur's bosom, if ever man went to Arthur's bosom. A made a finer end, and went away an it had been any christom child. A parted ev'n just between twelve and one, ev'n at the turning o'

th' tide: for after I saw him fumble with the sheets, and play with flowers, and smile upon his fingers' end, I knew there was but one way. For his nose was as sharp as a pen, and a babbled of green fields. 'How now, Sir John?' quoth I. 'What, man! Be o' good cheer.' So a cried out, 'God, God, God,' three or four times. Now I, to comfort him, bid him a should not think of God; I hoped there was no need to trouble himself with any such thoughts yet. So a bade me lay more clothes on his feet. I put my hand into the bed and felt them, and they were as cold as any stone. Then I felt to his knees, and they were as cold as any stone, and so up'ard and up'ard, and all was as cold as any stone.   (2.3.9–25)

The tenderness of Mistress Quickly's semi-articulacy in this multifaceted serio-comic anecdote shows Shakespeare's exceptional ability to combine satire with pathos in a profoundly humane manner. (Here, as occasionally elsewhere – I think especially of the orchard scenes in *Henry IV, Part Two* – he anticipates Chekhov.)

Shakespeare was skilful too in arousing laughter by devising situations of contrived discomfiture. Think for example of the brilliant episode in *Love's Labour's Lost* (4.1) in which Lord Biron tricks his three friends, the King, Lord Dumaine, and Lord Longueville, who have sworn to abjure the society of women, into revealing that they, like him, have fallen in love and into successively reading aloud the poems they have addressed to their mistresses, thus revealing their apostasy. I vividly recall the mounting and delighted glee of a young girl in the audience of a production long ago as she wriggled in her seat, stuffing a handkerchief into her mouth to stifle her laughter as she anticipated the successful outcome of Biron's trick. And there are similar episodes in later plays, such as the more emotionally loaded overhearing scenes in *Much Ado About Nothing* (2.3 and 3.1), *Troilus and Cressida* (5.2), and, in a tragic vein, in *Othello* (4.1) and *King Lear* (2.1).

Another way in which Shakespeare raises laughter is by devising situations in which, for example, a character may make a fool of himself or may be comically embarrassed as a result sometimes of accident, at other times by having a trick played upon him, as, in *Twelfth Night*, when Malvolio is deluded into supposing that his employer, Countess Olivia, is in love with him (2.5), or, more seriously, when Paroles is tricked into revealing his cowardice in *All's Well That Ends Well* (4.3). But it is characteristic of Shakespeare's ability to let us see situations in the round, as it were, from multiple points of view, that Malvolio is allowed his comeback – 'I'll be revenged on the whole pack of you' (5.1.374) – and that Paroles rapidly recovers his sangfroid with

> Captain I'll be no more.
> But I will eat and drink and sleep as soft
> As captain can. Simply the thing I am
> Shall make me live.   (4.3.332–335)

And a trick may result not just in comic discomfiture but in a significant gain in self-knowledge, as in *Much Ado About Nothing* when both Benedick and Beatrice successively are tricked into believing – or into acknowledging – that the other is in love with them.

16 Stephen Fry as Malvolio wearing yellow stockings (*Twelfth Night*, 3.4.15). Stephen played the role in an all-male production directed by Tim Carroll at Shakespeare's Globe in 2012. Mark Rylance played Olivia. When Stephen tweeted that I was in the audience, my number of followers increased significantly.

Shakespeare clearly takes pleasure in depicting episodes in which pomposity is deflated by wit: 'I can call spirits from the vasty deep,' says Glyndŵr in *Henry IV, Part One*. 'Why, so can I, or so can any man; / But will they come when you do call for them?' is Hotspur's riposte (3.1.51–2). And sometimes he raises laughter by comic business that does not depend on words. I think for example of Falstaff's appearance in disguise as the Old Woman of Brentford, in *The Merry Wives of Windsor* (4.2), or the carefully prepared-for appearance of Malvolio wearing cross-gartered yellow stockings in *Twelfth Night* (3.4).

One could go on, but it seems appropriate to end these chapters with some sort of summing up, an attempt at a character sketch of the man who himself 'created', as we say, such a memorable gallery of characters who have enriched the imaginations of readers and theatregoers over the centuries since his own imagination – stimulated, as we have seen, by many writings on which he was able to draw and also by his own acute powers of perception – brought them to imaginative life. So I end with a last attempt to answer the question with which I began: 'What was Shakespeare really like?'

I see Shakespeare as an essentially modest man, even humble, unflamboyant in his way of life, lacking personal vanity. His genius was at the service of his art. He was a team player, working with the same company of actors pretty well throughout his career, and serving his colleagues' needs as well as his own. No doubt he enjoyed the applause of the audiences who came to see his plays. He must have rejoiced in the company's many appearances at the court of Queen Elizabeth I and in their appointment when King James came to the throne, in 1603, as the King's Men, an acknowledgement of their status as the leading theatre company in the land. During his active career he had little concern for his literary reputation. He was a man of the theatre rather than a man of letters. We can say this because – unlike some of his contemporaries – Ben Jonson is a conspicuous example – he did not seek any form of publication for his plays other than performance. Only about half of his plays appeared in print during his lifetime and he seems to have had nothing to do with their publication.

That Shakespeare was a hard-working man is beyond doubt. I hope this is obvious not just from his consistent productivity but also from what I said about the amount of sheer hard work that went into the composition of his plays. And their intellectual and imaginative scope, especially in the later part of his career, shows that he was both intellectually and artistically ambitious, never content to rest on his laurels, but continually experimenting, stretching both himself and his audiences.

In his private life I think that by natural instinct Shakespeare was a family man. At various points in his career he provided amply for the welfare of both his immediate and his extended family through very substantial investments in property and land in Stratford-upon-Avon, not least – but not only – the purchase and development of New Place from 1597. From around 1604, it seems likely that he spent more time in Stratford than in London. His will, made in 1616 a couple of months before his death, is very much centred on his hometown. He makes careful and ample provision for the welfare of his sister, his daughters, and his granddaughter. Legacies to friends and neighbours demonstrate his commitment in his final years to the community into which he had been born. But during his working years he had not taken an active interest – as his father had for at least part of his

life – in municipal affairs. His attitude to the Welcombe enclosures suggests that in this instance an instinct for self-pro-
tection overcame more altruistic impulses.

Shakespeare is, I believe, the only playwright of his
time not to base himself entirely in London. But whatever
his devotion to Stratford-upon-Avon and to his family, his
profession as actor, playwright, and theatrical entrepreneur
required that he spend much of his time in the capital. During the 1590s, and later, he seems to have moved several times
from one dwelling to another. Did he do his own laundry?
Maybe Mrs Mountjoy, in whose household he lodged in the
early seventeenth century, was a motherly sort of person
who looked after the material welfare of her lodgers. Did she
cook for him? More seriously, where did he do his writing?
Most of it didn't come straight out of his head, in the way that
Keats sat down in his garden one morning and wrote 'Ode to
a Nightingale'. Shakespeare needed books, he needed a desk,
an inkwell, and a reliable supply of quill pens. In some plays,
such as *Henry V* and *Antony and Cleopatra*, it's clear that he
had a big book – Holinshed's *Chronicles*, Plutarch's *Lives* –
open before him as he wrote. Well, I suppose Mrs Mountjoy's kitchen table might have served, but I find it easier to
imagine him writing in the study at New Place in the relative peace and quiet of Stratford, especially while the theatres
were closed for long periods during bouts of plague.

He had no permanent address in London. This is
why one could call him our first great literary commuter. He
surely owned a horse, which would have required stabling, to
take him to and from Stratford. Sonnets 50 and 51 are written as it were on horseback and may recall his journeying

17 Shakespeare's gravestone and epitaph. His gravestone curiously bears no name, only the inscription traditionally ascribed to him:

Good friend, for Jesus' sake forbear
To dig the dust enclosed here.
Blessed be the man that spares these stones,
And cursed be he that moves my bones.

between Stratford-upon-Avon and London. In the first of them he bemoans the distance that he is putting between himself and his unidentified friend, and in the second he looks forward to spurring his horse towards the friend. In his journey between Stratford and London (surely a time when he was composing lines, speeches, and plots in his head), and as he walked between his London lodgings and the theatre, he would have had ample opportunity to observe and reflect

108

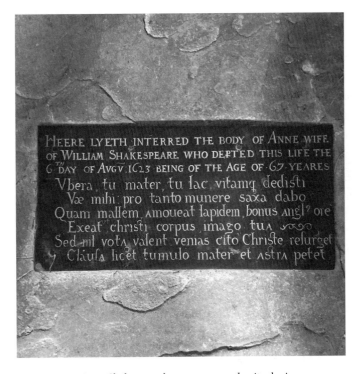

18 Anne Shakespeare's gravestone and epitaph. Anne Shakespeare, née Hathaway, died in 1623, seven years after her husband. The gravestone lies directly below his monument, suggesting that the plot was deliberately reserved for her. Translated from the Latin it reads: 'Mother, thou gavest me the breast, thou gavest me milk and life. Woe's me, for so great a gift my return will be but a tomb. Would that the good Angel would roll away the stone from its mouth, that thy form, like the body of Christ, might come forth! Yet are my prayers of no avail: O Christ, come quickly, that my mother, even though shut in the tomb, may rise again and seek the stars.'

upon the behaviour of the men and women he encountered, gathering material for his portrayal of the great gallery of human beings who people his plays.

What did he do for recreation? He was, surely, a musical man, as we can see from direct references to music in the Sonnets as well as the plays. And the churches as well as the theatres of his time resounded with great music. But he seems to have found time, too, for less high-minded pursuits. The anecdote from the diary of John Manningham that I quoted in my first chapter about Shakespeare taking Richard Burbage's place in a sexual assignation may seem too funny to be true, but it is enough to suggest that in the capital he had a reputation as a ladies' man.

Far more serious are the implications of the Sonnets. Not everyone shares my belief that by and large they are autobiographical. John Carey, for instance, in his *Little History of Poetry* (2020), writes that even though some of the sonnets 'seem clearly personal' still 'Shakespeare was a playwright. He spent his life making up speeches for imaginary people, and that is what these probably were' (p. 52). Well, as I hope I made clear in my chapter on these poems, I disagree. I am with Wordsworth, who wrote 'with this key / Shakespeare unlocked his heart'. And if we see the Sonnets as autobiographical then we must assume that their author had extramarital affairs, and that he was what we would now term bisexual.

I think Shakespeare had consummated love affairs with men and women and that he anguished over them in a manner that is displayed in some of his sonnets and reflected in the tormented self-laceration of, for example, Angelo in *Measure for Measure*. But I don't think Shakespeare entered into affairs at all lightly. The clearest evidence for his private, emotional, and sexual life derives from the Sonnets. Although some of them express anguish about passionate and deeply serious relationships with one or more women and men, none of them appear to express guilt about marital infidelity.

It looks as if he led a double life between Stratford and London. Whether his wife knew about this, and if so whether it mattered to her, we simply don't know. This is the premise of Ben Elton's script for Kenneth Branagh's 2019 film *All Is True*, though Elton portrays Shakespeare as being away from Stratford for much longer periods of time than I find plausible. Wherever Shakespeare was, he lived a life of abounding imaginative creativity. His nature was, as he himself writes in Sonnet 111, 'subdued' to what it worked in, 'like the dyer's hand'. He was able, with what John Keats – who understood him to his depths – calls his 'negative capability', to live what Keats also called 'a life of allegory'. We can hope best to know and understand him not through an account of the material facts of his life but through the writings, which record an imaginative and spiritual journey more vividly and profoundly than those of any other writer.

What of Shakespeare's religious sensibilities? Outwardly he appears to have been a conforming Christian. He and his family were baptized into the Christian faith, married into it, and were buried according to its rites. A number of his sonnets show a deep awareness of the transience of human life, sadness because 'that churl death my bones shall cover' (No. 32), and in *Measure for Measure* he vividly juxtaposes the Duke's Christian consolation 'Be absolute for death' with Claudio's horror of going 'we know not where … To lie in cold obstruction, and to rot' (3.1. 67–68). In his later plays especially he shows profound concern with mortality. In the final scene of *Hamlet* Horatio hopes that 'flights of angels' may sing the Prince to his rest, but *King Lear* offers no such consolations. In that play's closing moments the old enfeebled King, cradling his dead daughter in his arms, poses the ultimate existential question: 'Why should a dog, a horse, a rat have life, / And thou no breath at all?' The later plays, however, may suggest some degree of resolution, or at least of resignation. Prospero ends *The Tempest* by asking the audience to pray for him:

> And my ending is despair
> Unless I be relieved by prayer,
> Which pierces so that it assaults
> Mercy itself, and frees all faults.   (Epilogue)

So maybe the plays – especially the tragedies and the late romances – along with their consistent aim to entertain and engage the audiences of his time, also chart a spiritual journey. Again I find an analogy with the great composers, especially Beethoven and Schubert, whose works demonstrate ever-deepening levels of engagement with the most fundamental concerns of the human condition.

I think I've made it clear that I see Shakespeare as essentially a private man in spite of the public nature of his profession. He could put on a show of sociability, could work as one of a company, could mingle with his fellow actors and with the members of the aristocracy and the intelligentsia who attended performances at court. But he needed privacy for reading and thinking, and, prosperous though he became, he was content to live modestly in London while maintaining an establishment befitting the holder of a coat of arms in his hometown. He must, I think, have been a pretty self-sufficient man, able to fend for himself.

It seems likely, judging from how many plays he wrote, that Shakespeare enjoyed good health for most of his life. The fact that from around 1607 he started collaborating again with younger authors, first with the satirist and tragedian Thomas Middleton, then with the more romantically inclined John Fletcher, with whom he probably felt a clear imaginative sympathy, may suggest a dwindling creative impulse; and I suspect that the burning down of the Globe in 1613 had a traumatic effect.

Finally, we might ask ourselves: what is it that makes so many people think of Shakespeare as the greatest of writers? Partly it is his craftsmanship, grounded in an intellectual mastery of the principles of his profession. Partly it is his ever-developing powers of linguistic expression, ranging from complex rhetoric to the clear-talking simplicity of some of his most powerful utterances, which enable him to give voice with sympathy and admiration to an extraordinarily wide range of characters. And this is grounded in a profound imaginative understanding of his fellow human beings, enabling the characters of his plays to speak with their individual voices, free from judgement.

It is a long journey from *The Two Gentlemen of Verona* to *The Tempest*, a journey that takes us through courtship and marriage, through battles and warfare. I think Shakespeare's depth of feeling, his need for friendship and for love, results from a need to understand and to forgive himself. He was, as we can see from the Sonnets, 'desperately mortal', like Barnardine in *Measure for Measure* (4.2.147). He could say, like Richard II, 'I live with bread, like you; feel want, / Taste grief, need friends' (3.2.171–172). But he had, too, a sense also of the ideal, the possibility of transcendence, that though we 'golden lads and girls all must, / As chimney-sweepers, come to dust' (*Cymbeline* 4.2.263–264), yet there is hope. And in *The Winter's Tale* Hermione's apparent statue returns to life because Leontes awakes his faith. It is because Shakespeare was so much 'of an age', so deeply immersed in the life of his time, so vulnerable to temptation and open to experience, that he is also, as Ben Jonson put it, 'for all time'.

Epilogue: Eight Decades with Shakespeare – and More

❦

I have been going to see performances of Shakespeare's plays since the 1940s, and have seen most of the plays many times, in a wide range of production styles, on film and television as well as on the stage. I have seen some of them played in French, in German, in Swedish, in Romanian, in Hungarian, in Polish, in Greek, in Japanese, in Chinese, and in Russian. I have seen them given in pure and in heavily adapted texts. Early in my career I was a schoolmaster, struggling with the problems of making Shakespeare understandable, and if possible enjoyable, to the young. Later I taught Shakespeare in universities both in England and overseas. On being appointed director of the Shakespeare Institute of the University of Birmingham I became, I believe, the first ever Professor of Shakespeare Studies – there are quite a lot of them now. I have served as a governor and vice chairman of the Royal Shakespeare Company, as a trustee and council member of Shakespeare's Globe, as a trustee of the Rose Theatre and of Shakespeare's Birthplace, of which I have also been chairman and am now honorary president. I have organized summer schools on Shakespeare and taught on summer schools on Shakespeare. I have written books on

Shakespeare, reviewed books on Shakespeare, reported on Shakespeare books for publishers, and even read books on Shakespeare without having to review or report on them. For nineteen years I edited the annual *Shakespeare Survey*, published by Cambridge University Press. I have lectured on Shakespeare in many countries of the world. I have studied imitations of Shakespeare and parodies of Shakespeare, I have made speeches about Shakespeare, I have presented (and, if I may say so in all modesty), received awards and prizes to do with Shakespeare, I have judged competitions and debates about Shakespeare, written letters to newspapers about Shakespeare, sat on committees to do with Shakespeare, spoken about Shakespeare on radio and on television, eaten meals and drunk toasts in honour of Shakespeare, answered innumerable queries from all and sundry about Shakespeare, blogged and tweeted about Shakespeare, and one hot summer day I spent ten hours on trains to get to a school in Wales in order to inaugurate what was called a 'bardathon' – a reading aloud by schoolboys of the complete works of Shakespeare which continued for another four days and nights after I had happily left the stalwart participants to get on with it.

In view of all this it is no doubt understandable that I sometimes get asked whether I am never bored with Shakespeare, whether the concentration of my professional, and even at times of my personal life on this single author has not induced a sense of satiety, a desire to move on to something completely different. Happily for me, the answer is no. I can't honestly say that Shakespeare figured largely during the first decade of my life. In fact I don't remember having had the faintest idea of who he was during those innocent years. It was not until my second decade, when I moved from the local primary school to a grammar school (in Hull, East Yorkshire) at the age of eleven, that my initiation took place. I have a vague memory of an English lesson with a Mr Woolf during which I stood in front of the class brandishing a ruler in what must have been the enactment of one of the battle scenes in *Julius Caesar*. I remember also a reading round the class of *A Midsummer Night's Dream* in which I felt a priggish frisson at having to speak the word 'hell' in Hermia's line 'O hell – to choose love by another's eyes.' (We were an innocent lot then.) But it was a few years later, when I was an adolescent beginning to feel the first pangs of love, that I began to be deeply stirred by Shakespeare's language. This was, naturally enough, in one of the sonnets, not in a play – Sonnet 29, the one beginning 'When, in disgrace with fortune and men's eyes' and ending 'For thy sweet love remembered such wealth brings / That then I scorn to change my state with kings'. It remains a favourite.

Around this time too I began to see the plays acted. The great barnstorming actor Sir Donald Wolfit used to tour the provinces with a somewhat undistinguished company. Even he himself was not always on top form. I remember him lying on the floor of the stage having a fit as Othello, his hands drumming the floor while his eyes surveyed the house anxiously checking how many people there were in the audience. And at the close of *Hamlet* he came on to take his call hanging wearily on to the curtains and wiping the sweat off his brow as, using Hamlet's words, he declared 'Beggar that I am, I am even poor in thanks; but I thank you'. But at his best, especially as King Lear, he was a great actor.

My pleasure in seeing Shakespeare acted was in part the reason for my choosing to go to University College London, as an undergraduate, and while there I was able to see many memorable performances, including Laurence Olivier as Richard III, Olivier and Vivien Leigh as Antony and Cleopatra, Alec Guinness as Hamlet (on my twenty-first birthday), and Peggy Ashcroft as Viola. In those days the academic world took little professional interest in Shakespearean performance. I remember telling my tutor, a fine literary critic of Shakespeare, that I was going to see Michael Redgrave play Hamlet. 'O,' she said, 'I should like to see *Hamlet*. Some time.' The first ever British university drama department had started, at Bristol, only the year before I went up to university. All the best historians of the British theatre at that time were American – I think especially of my old friend Arthur Colby Sprague, and of Charles Shattuck. In the decades since then, of course, theatre-based criticism has escalated until it is now a whole sub-branch of the industry – and one to which I, along with many of my colleagues, have contributed. It's also strange to think that when I went to UCL only five books had been published in English on the subject of Shakespeare's comedies since those plays were written. There are now many hundreds.

In the third decade of my life, when I worked as a schoolmaster, I became acutely aware of the difficulties in bringing Shakespeare to life for young people. It's a perennial problem and one to which there are no easy solutions. It's easy enough to do the externals – to tell young people what we know about Shakespeare's life, to take them to the Birthplace and the other Shakespeare houses so that they may gain a sense of his social and cultural environment, to introduce them to the basic stories of the plays, perhaps reading to and with them Leon Garfield's excellent modern prose retellings of them (not *Lamb's Tales*, in my view – far too sentimental and dated) – or showing them the series of half-hour *Animated Tales from Shakespeare* produced initially for Welsh television, on which I acted as academic adviser around the start of my sixth decade, an occupation which took me several times to Moscow, where the films were made. These

19 The Prospero puppet. The puppets used in the *Animated Tales* version of *The Tempest* were no more than a few inches high. The half-hour film was made in Moscow on a table top. Prospero was modelled in part on Stanley Wells.

use Shakespeare's own words, though obviously in heavily curtailed form, so they also serve as an introduction to his language. Curiously, it was only recently I learnt that the Russian animator based the puppet cast as Prospero on me.

It's fair enough, in my opinion, to get young students to learn selected passages by heart, and even to read with them more or less self-contained extracts, such as the witches' scenes from *Macbeth*, or filleted versions of individual plays – perhaps the Shylock scenes from *The Merchant of Venice*, or the taming scenes from *The Taming of the Shrew*. Of course it's important to inculcate a sense of the play's theatricality, not an easy thing to do in the classroom. Any teacher who can persuade children that Falstaff is funny just by reading the play cold is a genius. You can give them more of a sense of the plays' potential impact by taking them to see a theatre performance, preferably not sitting all together, which is liable to reduce them to the lowest common denominator of response and behaviour, but distributed widely among the audience like civilized human beings. But the productions must be good. I remember when I was a schoolmaster, in my third decade, taking a fifth-year class to see a matinee performance of *Henry IV, Part One*, which they were studying, in a great barn of a theatre in Portsmouth. It was FA Cup Final day, and we were almost the only members of the audience. Falstaff was played by an old, once great actor who was far past his best. In fact he was wearing a hearing aid, and it was not a deliberate part of the characterization of the role. We might as well have stayed at home and listened to the football match on the radio.

In the early 2000s the Royal Shakespeare Company ran a campaign called 'Stand Up for Shakespeare', which made strident and authoritarian claims for the merits of plunging children straight into the action by getting them on their feet and acting the roles with no previous preparation. This may work with some children for some scenes of some plays, but it ignores the fact that some children are less extrovert than others, and perhaps more importantly that Shakespeare is not only a dramatist but also our greatest poet and a profound thinker, whose writings can give as much pleasure on the page as on the stage, and whose language at times requires deep study rather than simply to be rattled off with more concern for immediacy of effect than for depth of understanding. I feel a bit conflicted about this: for much of my life I have been insisting that Shakespeare was above all a practical dramatist, and that his plays can only be fully understood in performance; but at the present time I'm beginning to fear that overemphasis on his theatrical accessibility is leading towards a populist approach which stresses superficiality over depth.

By the time I had entered my fourth decade I had moved to Stratford-upon-Avon where I took my PhD at the Shakespeare Institute of the University of Birmingham in 1962. This came about because I had done a couple of weeks' voluntary work there in 1958, at the end of which the founder and then director, Allardyce Nicoll, a great historian of the English drama who became a significant mentor, asked me if I would like to apply for a scholarship. I did so, got it, and, not really having much awareness of the research scene, was drafted into editing for my dissertation – or thesis, as we more usually called it then – two rather boring works by Robert Greene. In doing so I developed a taste for editorial work which was to have a great impact on the rest of my professional life. I became a Fellow of the Institute, and started to work closely with Nicoll's successor as director, Terence Spencer. I collaborated with him on the new edition of Shakespeare that he was invited to prepare for Penguin Books and in doing so gained insights into the editorial process and, no less importantly, into the working habits of editors of scholarly works. Spencer was a fine classical scholar and a considerable wit who abhorred intellectual pretension and was a brilliant communicator. These qualities made him an ideal choice as general editor of a new Shakespeare edition to be published by Penguin Books, with their ideals of high intellectual quality combined with lucidity and accessibility. He assembled an experienced team of editorial advisers, many of whom had edited plays for scholarly series such as the Arden Shakespeare and the Revels Plays. The New Penguin would aim to serve a broader readership beyond that of scholars and graduate students, aiming to make the most recent scholarship and the best current critical thought accessible to younger students, actors, and what we would refer to as 'the Penguin reader' – intelligent laypersons with no previous specialized knowledge.

Existing editions in the early sixties had failed to keep up with the times. As I have mentioned, in the postwar period scholars had at last woken up to the fact that the theatre might have something to tell them, indeed that performance is itself a form of criticism, and that actors and their directors may have insights into the text that are no less valuable than those of literary scholars and critics. But J. Dover Wilson's idiosyncratic and often eccentric New Cambridge edition, then dragging painfully towards its close, paid only token tribute to the theatre in its bare, completely uncritical lists of productions through the ages, and the ongoing Arden edition of those days paid even less attention to performance. Penguin Books organized a one-day conference in Stratford attended by a dozen or so scholars and led by Spencer aiming to discuss the principles on which a new edition might best be prepared, and we talked for hours about many aspects of editing. Some of the decisions at which we eventually arrived represented reactions against current practice. For instance, many of the Arden editions opened forbiddingly with a dry-as-dust discussion of the play's date of composition followed by equally uninspiring accounts of textual problems, topical allusions, sources, and so on, leaving critical discussion to the end. It was all representative of a hierarchical, teacher-knows-best, facts-are-good-for-you attitude toward the reader. We wanted the New Penguin to be more engaging, not merely to present information but to show our readers why it would be worth their while to take an interest in it, how it might help them to engage with a play's most serious concerns. So it was decided that our introductions should incorporate this kind of information into essays that made imaginative critical use of factual material rather than just handing it to readers on a plate with a take-it-or leave-it attitude. We spent hours talking about whether the notes should be at the foot of the page, as in the Arden, or at the end of the book, as in the New Cambridge. We wanted to give our readers access to scholarly information without making them feel that it was being forced down their throats. So finally we decided to place annotative material at the back of the book. It was, I'm sure, the right decision, and one that has helped to give the edition, now published with new introductions with myself and Paul Edmondson in charge, its ongoing popularity. Many actors have told me that they like it if only because the clean page allows them space to write their own notes in the margins.

My own position in all this was initially very much that of an acolyte, an attendant lord – or even commoner – listening respectfully to his seniors and only occasionally tentatively venturing a suggestion. Once the edition got underway I acted as a general dogsbody, corresponding with editors on Spencer's behalf, reading and checking typescripts – no printouts in those days – as they came in, helping to iron out inconsistencies of presentation with our superb copy-editor, Judith Wardman, and reading proofs. I was a kind of Ariel to Spencer's Prospero, even at times a somewhat mischievous Puck to his Oberon. At first my work went unacknowledged, but things took a turn for the better one day when I was standing next to the Penguin director responsible for it all, Charles Clark. 'I think you'd better have some official share in all this,' he said, and that's how I came to be acknowledged as associate editor and to be given a small but very welcome financial interest in the edition. Spencer generously invited me to take responsibility for a play myself, and I chose *A Midsummer Night's Dream* – always one of my favourites. This was followed in later years by *The Comedy of Errors* and *Richard II*. And after Spencer's premature death I, along with Anne Barton, undertook the melancholy task of completing his unfinished edition of *Hamlet*.

Towards the close of my fifth decade a senior editor at Oxford University Press, aware of my work on the New Penguin edition and of other relevant experience, invited me to assume the general editorship of a new edition of the Complete Works. The then existing Oxford Shakespeare, edited by W. J. Craig, had appeared as long ago as 1891, and in the meantime many important discoveries about Shakespeare's text had been made. OUP's efforts to replace Craig's edition by commissioning scholars who would work on it while occupying a full-time university appointment had failed, but it was a bold move to establish a full-time Shakespeare department with me at its head, to be joined later by Gary Taylor, John Jowett, and William Montgomery. Soon after my move to Oxford I was appointed to a senior research fellowship at Balliol College, a move which helped to keep me in touch with university affairs. Not long after this I assumed the editorship of *Shakespeare Survey*, established by my old mentor Allardyce Nicoll, and published by the rival Cambridge University Press, which I was to edit for the next nineteen years.

When I first started to tell people in Oxford that I was to edit a new edition of the Complete Works, the information was liable to be received with a very Oxfordian curl of the upper lip accompanied by a raising of the left eyebrow along with the question 'O, will it be any different from all the other editions?' Condescension turned to consternation in some quarters when it turned out to be very different indeed. I felt strongly that there was no point in adopting a timid conservatism that shied away from the application of hypotheses which, though they might be unprovable, had behind them the weight of sound scholarship and rational thought. Knowing that the almost invariable practice in previous editions of the Complete Works from the First Folio onwards – Edward Capell's is the honourable exception – had been to mark up an earlier version, leaving many of the conventions of presentation including the spelling, punctuation, capitalization, and even editorial stage directions to stand without new thought, I was determined that we should work from the original quartos and the First Folio to produce a text that was genuinely designed for the modern reader, rethinking conventions of presentation from the ground upwards, and that we should act on the best modern thought even when it challenged orthodoxy. There was a fashion at the time, exemplified for instance by Philip Edwards's edition of the plays of Philip Massinger and Fredson Bowers's of Thomas Dekker and of the Beaumont and Fletcher canon, to edit plays of the period in old spelling, but this was not what I had been appointed to do. My first self-appointed task after I had accepted the job was to write a detailed study of the principles and practice of modernizing Shakespeare's spelling – a topic which had never over the centuries been the subject of serious scholarly consideration. I came to the conclusion that it should be thorough. As a result, to give only a few examples, in the Oxford edition Ancient Iago becomes Ensign Iago, Petruchio – spelt in the First Folio with a *c h* and therefore often pronounced in an unItalian fashion as Petruckio – becomes Petruccio (with a double *c*, pronounced as in 'clutch'), the Forest of Arden becomes the forest of Ardenne, and Glendower is given his proper Welsh spelling.

Fresh thought about conventions of presentation such as these affects only details of the text, but it does so at many points. More radical was our decision to act upon what I see as the two most significant, indeed revolutionary, developments in thought about Shakespeare's text of the past few decades. The first of these, adumbrated by Ernst Honigmann in his seminal 1965 book *The Stability of Shakespeare's Text* – which is actually about the instability of Shakespeare's text – is the recognition that some of Shakespeare's plays survive in both unrevised and revised forms, that the traditionally conflated texts of plays such as *Hamlet* and *King Lear* are neither one thing nor the other, and that the only proper scholarly procedure is to edit each version in its own right. In this policy we were acting on ideas that were being thrashed out only as we were working, and that indeed we ourselves – especially Gary Taylor – were helping to develop. Also, since Shakespeare was so much a practical man of the theatre, it seemed proper to give priority to the revised versions representing these plays as acted in the theatre of his time rather than to the texts as they first came from his pen, however fascinating his earlier thoughts might be. As a consequence we printed, for example, a Folio-based text of *Hamlet* which does not include in the body of the text quarto-only passages such as, most conspicuously, Hamlet's last soliloquy, 'How all occasions do inform against me'. There is one play, *King Lear*, for which we printed two separate texts, one based on the quarto, the other on the Folio, because the differences are so great as to represent two different plays. If we had been working a few years later we should probably have printed both quarto- and Folio-based versions of, at least, *Othello*, *Troilus and Cressida*, and *Hamlet*.

Our decision to prioritize texts as acted in Shakespeare's theatre led to the single most controversial feature of our edition, one that sent shock waves all round the world when it first appeared, which was to call Falstaff in *Henry IV,*

Part One by the name he first appeared on stage, that is, Old-castle, which we know was changed to Falstaff as the result of protests from Oldcastle's descendants. It was a bold, perhaps even foolhardy decision but one that I still can't regret – there are after all many hundreds of editions of the play where you can read it with the name Falstaff, and it didn't seem all that wicked to provide the first and only one where you can read it with the name as Shakespeare first intended it to appear. I think that if the name had appeared thus in an edition published by a minority press it would have been hailed as a brilliantly bold step rather than reviled as a desecration as some people regarded it in an Oxford text.

The second (in point of time) most important development in Shakespeare studies of the past few decades is the recognition that a number of plays from early and late in his career were written in collaboration with other writers. This is an ongoing topic which has been further developed since our edition appeared, but in the Oxford Shakespeare *Henry VI, Part One* is ascribed to William Shakespeare and Others, *Macbeth* and *Timon of Athens* to Shakespeare and Middleton, *Pericles* to Shakespeare and George Wilkins, and *Henry VIII* (under its original title of *All Is True*) as by Shakespeare and Fletcher, all of which ascriptions have been supported by later scholarship.

Our radicalism extended too to a rethinking of the canon, most notoriously in the inclusion of a harmless little lyric beginning 'Shall I die ...', which is plainly ascribed to William Shakespeare in a seventeenth-century manuscript. Its inclusion scandalized some of our colleagues beyond all reason.

20 Stanley Wells with the first copy of *The Oxford Shakespeare: The Complete Works* (1986), outside the chapel of Balliol College, Oxford.

The edition first appeared in 1986, sadly (for financial reasons) without the glossarial and other notes that we had written as we worked. A second edition, which includes *Edward III* and the full text, rather than just the Shakespearean portions, of *Sir Thomas More* was published in 2005. The Oxford Shakespeare is very much a stage-oriented edition, but actors naturally prefer to work from something more portable. One of my regrets is that the plays as we edited them have not been published separately in a more portable form that would have made them more useful to actors. I often groan inwardly – and sometimes even outwardly – when I hear actors attempting to reproduce vocally archaic spellings, such as 'y'are', which are preserved in other editions but modernized in ours.

The publication of the Oxford edition in 1986 represented the culmination of a significant phase in my life. To that extent it was a cause for celebration, but it had the unfortunate effect of making me jobless. I spent a few difficult months wondering how I should continue to earn a living, but then, happily for me, the directorship of the Shakespeare Institute, where I had worked for much of the earlier part of my career, fell vacant. I was appointed to the position and to the newly created chair of Shakespeare Studies. This was a time when Shakespeare's global influence was coming increasingly to be felt. I was made keenly aware of this in 1987 during the period of perestroika when I was one of a group of Shakespeare scholars – Peter Holland was another – invited to Moscow for the first international Shakespeare event to be held since the start of the Communist era. The conference itself had political significance. We saw a performance of *Hamlet* which was clearly subversive in intent, and heard about other productions in which the voice of protest had, however covertly, made itself heard.

But my most dramatic contact with political events of world significance came in 1989, towards the close of my sixth decade, when the British Council invited me to visit Czechoslovakia, as it then was, with as my host its senior Shakespearean, Zdeněk Stříbrný, who for years had been forbidden to teach because of his liberal views. I arrived on 19 November, and as I was being shown round the castle area Zdeněk told me there had been what he called 'a spot of bother' – police had beaten up some students, one of whom was rumoured – falsely, as it later emerged – to have died. On the following day my lecture to the Czech Academy was punctuated throughout by the rhythmical chanting of a vast procession of protesters winding their way from Wenceslaus Square to the presidential palace. Afterwards I stood on a balcony with members of the audience to watch the seemingly endless procession stream by, the walkers waving up to the tall plate-glass windows of the National Theatre, which faces the Academy. Actors, who I was told had, along with the students, been instrumental in orchestrating the protest, waved back. As the days passed, more and more processions of workers from the provinces marched through the streets. I still have the badge bearing an image of the playwright Václav Havel which was thrown down from a window as I joined the crowds thronging the streets to see him and Alexander Dubček address the vast assembly that packed Wenceslaus Square.

Towards the end of my seventh decade, when I was in my sixties, the time came for me to retire from my professorial chair, a milestone marked at the Shakespeare Institute by a special, open-air student production of *A Midsummer Night's Dream*, a play that has meant much to me since my first, classroom encounter with it. In this production the students had engineered a special, surprise appearance by my younger daughter, Clemency, as First Fairy. It was not her natural métier. Indeed she admitted afterwards that she hated every moment of it and did it only for my sake, which of course I found very touching.

Although retirement meant that I could no longer base myself at the Shakespeare Institute, with which I had been closely associated for close on four decades, I was fortunate to be already chairman of the Shakespeare Birthplace Trust, and was delighted to be offered the use of an office at their headquarters where I have been able to continue with many of my other activities as well as taking part in those of the Trust. Release from full-time teaching meant that I could devote more time to writing, and I spent the first three years of my retirement mostly on preparing an edition of *King Lear* for the multivolume Oxford Shakespeare, of which I was general editor. It was a symptom of the late twentieth-century shift in thought about Shakespeare's texts that I based my edition firmly on the quarto – partly because this version of the play had not been edited in its own right. And in my eighth decade I was able to publish several books, in one of which, *Shakespeare and Co.*, I write about Shakespeare in relation to the other dramatists of his time. I've always enjoyed collaborating with other scholars – long ago with Robert Smallwood, on our Revels edition of *The Shoemaker's Holiday*, Gary Taylor and others on the Oxford Shakespeare, Margreta de Grazia on Cambridge Companions, and especially in recent years with Paul Edmondson, in books and a number of co-authored articles and talks as well as a little *jeu d'esprit* published originally as *Coffee with Shakespeare* (2008; currently ranked 2,405,325 on Amazon). Also during this period I've kept sticking my neck out about a never-ending stream of new theories and supposed discoveries about Shakespeare. I've poured cold water on the idea that he had Lancashire connections and was a crypto-Catholic. I've pooh-poohed the idea that the contents of pipes found in Stratford show that he smoked cannabis. I've ridiculed the notion that he was murdered by his son-in-law, John Hall. I've disputed the view that Mr W. H. of the dedication to the Sonnets is a misprint for Mr W. S., standing for William Shakespeare, and also that he wrote a poem called 'A Funeral Elegy'. I've written a whole, rather jokey short book called *Is It True What They Say about Shakespeare?* (2007) in which I survey questions that are often raised and assess my responses to them.

On the other hand I have also defended other new theories, some of which have not had the full support of all my colleagues. Most notably, perhaps, I've stood up for the plausibility of the suggestion that the Jacobean portrait of an unidentified gentleman – the Cobbe portrait – may be the only surviving life portrait of Shakespeare and that it may have formed the basis for the Droeshout engraving. Indeed I collaborated with the art historian Alec Cobbe on a whole book about the topic and about Shakespeare's relations with his patron, the Earl of Southampton. The unveiling of the portrait in March 2009, towards the end of my eighth decade, attracted worldwide attention, with headlines and photographs in newspapers and on television screens all over the world. Predictably, and properly, it also attracted much scepticism. It is the duty of scholars to be sceptical. They also have a duty to examine all the evidence presented to them with scrupulous care. This did not always happen. Experts on Shakespeare (rather than art historians), dragged from their laptops by reporters avid for comment, were not slow to express doubt. Some of the objections relied on what I regard as false assumptions about Shakespeare's social status and the position of actors in Elizabethan society. Well, arguments about the painting are likely to continue, but one thing that no one questions is that, as even the most adversarial of our critics, Katherine Duncan-Jones, said, 'The Cobbe portrait is a splendid painting that depicts an exceptionally good-looking man of wit and wisdom, one of nature's observers, as Shakespeare surely was.' Though we cannot proclaim its authenticity with total assurance, it has established itself, along with the National Portrait Gallery's aesthetically inferior, badly damaged, and inadequately authenticated yet endlessly reproduced Chandos portrait, as the painting most likely to represent Shakespeare as he lived.

My involvement with Shakespearian controversy has continued into my ninth decade. Doubts about Shakespeare's authorship of his works have been expressed since at least 1856. Many of my colleagues have felt it beneath their dignity to respond, but I have often entered the arena and thrown my cloak in front of the bulls even at the risk of getting impaled on their horns. Over the years I've pleaded Shakespeare's cause on radio and television programmes, in a formal mock trial held at the Inner Temple where I was cross-examined by an eminent QC, Lord Alexander, with whom I was later to work closely when he was chairman and I vice chairman of the RSC. Prince Philip was a sceptic. For a time he supported the idea that the plays were written by a diplomat named Sir Henry Neville (1564–1615). My friend Sir Eric Anderson, headmaster of Eton College, knowing that I had debunked these claims in *Is It True?*, sent a copy to the Prince, but to no effect. When he visited Stratford with the Queen to open the rebuilt theatre in 2011, I somewhat cheekily said, 'So, sir, I hear you're still a sceptic.' 'Yes,' he replied, grinning, 'even more so after reading your book.'

More recently, provoked by the 2011 film *Anonymous*, which portrays Shakespeare as a drunken, illiterate, and almost inarticulate buffoon, a mere stooge for the Earl of Oxford, I have enjoyed working with Paul Edmondson in his capacity of Head of Research at the Shakespeare Birthplace Trust in a campaign in defence of Shakespeare. Together we devised questions for an online campaign, Sixty Minutes with Shakespeare, with many distinguished contributors, including Dame Margaret Drabble, Stephen Fry, Sir Antony Sher, and the then Prince of Wales (who did not subscribe to his father's views on the topic), all responding to questions relating to Shakespeare's authorship. Together too we have co-authored a free e-book, *Shakespeare Bites Back*, which has been downloaded over half a million times, and a collection of essays, *Shakespeare Beyond Doubt*, which we commissioned and edited and which appeared in 2013.

I look back over all my decades with Shakespeare with great gratitude for his continuing companionship, for the inspiration his writings have given me, for the friendships he has brought into my life, for the continuing fount of inspiration that I have derived from his works.

I had the excitement in 2010 of appearing before a large audience (who had, admittedly, come primarily to see Roger Allam play Falstaff in *Henry IV, Part One*) on the stage of Shakespeare's Globe to receive the Sam Wanamaker Award – a framed photograph of Sam – and no less excitingly to be awarded the Craiova Shakespeare Prize on the stage of the Romanian Festival Theatre there at the end of a performance by Propeller Theatre Company of *A Midsummer Night's Dream*. I received both a welcome cash gift and a trophy in the shape of a weighty bronze effigy of Shakespeare's head with slices carved out of it which got through customs only on the plea that it was 'a kind of Oscar'. It now sits on my honours table along with another metal trophy featuring a naked Hamlet gazing at a skull which was awarded by the Fundación Shakespeare Argentina during lockdown in 2020. And I'm also proud of the silver cup presented to me by three of my friends after I beat them all in a tensely fought game of clock golf on the banks of the Avon.

Other writings have appeared, including a couple of *Very Short Introductions* (2015 and 2017) in the Oxford University Press series and volumes co-written or co-edited with Paul Edmondson – *The Shakespeare Circle* (2015), and, more recently, *All the Sonnets of Shakespeare* (2020) in which for the first time the sonnets are printed (it was Paul's idea) in chronological order rather than that in which they first appeared, in 1609, and in which we intersperse them with passages in sonnet form from the plays. I think we can fairly claim that our book is having a major impact on thought about these great but often misunderstood poems.

Lighter-weight trophies than the Craiova bust include the nice medal on a silk ribbon I got on receiving a knighthood in 2016 ('after all these years, Stanley,' Prince Charles kindly said). I nearly didn't get it as the letter from the Prime Minister offering me the honour went astray; happily a phone call from his office to a hotel where I was staying with my daughters and granddaughter put matters straight. That was a thrill-packed year, aided by events in commemoration of the 400th anniversary of Shakespeare's death including a visit to Venice for a special performance of *The Merchant of Venice* in the Ghetto, which was celebrating its 500th anniversary. Most hilarious was my appearance on the television show *Cunk on Shakespeare*, where the comedienne Diane Morgan, alias Philomena Cunk, interviewed me about *Romeo and Juliet*. 'Shakespeare's tragedies,' she opined, 'are the most performed of all his works, none more so than *Hamlet*, with its famous speech about bees.' And 'School in Shakespeare's day and age was vastly different to our own. In fact, it was far easier because he didn't have to study Shakespeare.'

Teaching and discussion have continued. Since 2015 I've enjoyed taking part, along with the former Archbishop of Canterbury, Rowan Williams, and other scholars in an annual series of what are described as 'retreats' – a word which makes them sound more austere than they actually are – at Cumberland Lodge in Windsor Great Park: short courses in which over a period of four days groups of around forty individuals – they tend mostly to be clerics and medics – enjoy the generous hospitality of this great institution while discussing a single Shakespeare play in a series of lectures, seminars, and discussion groups.

In 2020, shortly before my ninetieth birthday, I had the privilege – and great pleasure – of appearing in conversation with my old friend Dame Judi Dench as the ninth of the Notre Dame London Shakespeare Lectures. Any event involving Judi is always a great deal of fun as well as a source of enlightenment. Shortly after that I enjoyed seeing Michael Pennington as Prospero in *The Tempest* at the Jermyn Street Theatre in London, but already storm clouds were gathering. A few days later the full onset of the pandemic brought an abrupt end to public events and has had a catastrophic effect on Stratford from which it will take years to recover. Needless to say, however, though I have been unable to see Shakespeare's plays acted in the theatre, I have continued to think and to write about him. Work on *All the Sonnets of Shakespeare* stimulated me to think more about Shakespeare as a man among men, one who, for all his genius and his towering reputation, 'in his nakedness' appeared, like his own Henry V (4.1.105), a vulnerable man, like the rest of us. And this thinking informed the lectures 'What Was Shakespeare Really Like?', which I completed and delivered online in the early days of the pandemic and which form the bulk of this book. Shakespeare has been my companion for most of my life. For this I am profoundly grateful.

BOOK LIST

All quotations from Shakespeare are taken from the Complete Works, edited by Stanley Wells, Gary Taylor, John Jowett, and William Montgomery (Oxford University Press, 1986; revised edition 2005).

The following is a selective list of books referred to in my lectures along with a few more that readers might find relevant and helpful.

Bradley, A. C., *Oxford Lectures on Poetry*. Oxford: Clarendon Press, 1909.

Bradley, A. C., *Shakespearian Tragedy: Lectures on* Hamlet, Othello, King Lear, Macbeth. London: Penguin, 1991; first published 1904.

Bullough, Geoffrey (ed.), *Narrative and Dramatic Sources of Shakespeare*. 8 vols. London: Routledge & Kegan Paul, 1957–1973.

Chambers, E. K., *William Shakespeare: A Study of Facts and Problems*. 2 vols. Oxford: Clarendon Press, 1930.

Crystal, David, and Ben Crystal, *Shakespeare's Words: A Glossary and Language Companion*. London: Penguin, 2002.

Dobson, Michael, and Stanley Wells (eds). *The Oxford Companion to Shakespeare*. Oxford University Press, 2001; revised edition, 2015.

Duncan-Jones, Katherine, *Ungentle Shakespeare: Scenes from His Life*. London: Arden Shakespeare, 2001; revised edition 2010.

Gillespie, Stuart, *Shakespeare's Books: A Dictionary of Shakespeare's Sources*. London: Athlone, 2001.

Gurr, Andrew, *Playgoing in Shakespeare's London*. Cambridge University Press, 2004.

Kermode, Frank, *Shakespeare's Language*. London: Allen Lane, 2000.

Munro, John (ed.), *The Shakspere Allusion Book: A Collection of Allusions to Shakspere from 1591–1700*. 2 vols. Oxford University Press, 1932.

Nicholl, Charles, *The Lodger: Shakespeare on Silver Street*. London: Allen Lane, 2007.

Schoenbaum, S. *William Shakespeare: A Compact Documentary Life*. Oxford: Clarendon Press, 1977.

Shaw, George Bernard, *Shaw on Shakespeare*, with an introduction by Edwin Wilson. Harmondsworth: Penguin, 1969.

Spurgeon, Caroline F. E., *Shakespeare's Imagery and What it Tells Us*. Cambridge University Press, 1935; reprinted 1993.

Also by Stanley Wells

Re-editing Shakespeare for the Modern Reader. Oxford University Press, 1979.

Shakespeare: A Dramatic Life. London: Sinclair-Stevenson, 1994, reprinted as *Shakespeare: A Life in Drama*, W. W. Norton, 1996.

The Oxford Companion to Shakespeare, edited with Michael Dobson. Oxford University Press, 2001; new edition 2015.

Shakespeare: For All Time. London: Macmillan, 2002.

Shakespeare's Sonnets, with Paul Edmondson. Oxford University Press, 2004.

Shakespeare and Co.: Christopher Marlowe, Thomas Dekker, Ben Jonson, Thomas Middleton, John Fletcher and the Other Players in His Story. London: Penguin Books, 2007.

Shakespeare in the Theatre: An Anthology of Criticism. Oxford University Press, 2007.

Looking for Sex in Shakespeare. Cambridge University Press, 2010.

Shakespeare, Sex and Love. Oxford University Press, 2010.

Great Shakespeare Actors: Burbage to Branagh. Oxford University Press, 2013.

Shakespeare Beyond Doubt: Evidence, Argument, Controversy, edited with Paul Edmondson. Cambridge University Press, 2013.

The Shakespeare Circle, edited with Paul Edmondson. Cambridge University Press, 2015.

INDEX

Page numbers in *italics* refer to content in figures.